W9-CZU-130

THE DEFECTIVE IMAGE

How Darwinism Fails to Provide an Adequate Account of the World

Ben M. Carter

University Press of America,® Inc.
Lanham · New York · Oxford

Copyright © 2001 by
University Press of America,® Inc.
4720 Boston Way
Lanham, Maryland 20706

12 Hid's Copse Rd.
Cumnor Hill, Oxford OX2 9JJ

British Library Cataloging in Publication Information Available

Library of Congress Cataloging-in-Publication Data

Carter, Ben M.
The defective image : how Darwinism fails to provide an
adequate account of the world / Ben M. Carter.
p.   cm
Includes bibliographical references and index.
1. Genetic psychology. 2. Human evolution. I. Title.
BF701 .C36   2001   146'.7—dc21   2001027003 CIP

ISBN 0-7618-1961-4 (cloth: alk. paper)

Every man is brutish in his knowledge: every
founder is confounded by the graven image ...

Jeremiah 10:14; 51:17

... it may not be a logical deduction, but to my
imagination it is far more satisfactory to look at
... instincts ... not as specially endowed or
created ..., but as small consequences of one
general law, leading to the advancement of all
organic beings, namely, multiply, vary, let the
strongest live and the weakest die.

Charles Darwin
The Origin of Species
Chapter 7 "Instinct," p. 201

This book is dedicated to
Mark and Brenda Atterberry
and Gene and Kathy Knaack

Table of Contents

Acknowledgments

Acknowledgments

This book was written between 1997 and 2000. It was occasioned by my own loss of "faith" in the theory of evolution, a loss that made me increasingly aware of the dogmatism of those who insist that Darwin's model is as fixed in the intellectual firmament as the heliocentric solar system. Earlier drafts of some of these chapters have appeared in the *Global Journal of Classical Theology*, the *Journal of Christian Apologetics*, and *Perspectives on Science and Christian Faith*. Others were delivered as papers at various conferences in the United States. In all cases I have received much instructive feedback for which I am most grateful and the fruits of which I hope are evident in this book. Also I have been privileged to dialogue with posters on the MSNBC science bulletin board, many of whom provided very challenging and insightful responses to the ideas herein expressed. In this regard I am particular thankful to the poster "Michael" who recommended several of the books to which I have referred in these pages. I am also indebted to Michael Darnell and Dr. Irene Hickman who, despite their often profound differences with me, were always gracious and read and critiqued earlier drafts of this book. I also wish to thank my father Ben W. Carter who proofread the text and in the process made invaluable suggestions, my mother Hilda M. Carter who, despite her own battle with cancer during these years, remained interested in this project and whose courage, already evidenced in her struggle with polio and post-polio, inspired me, and my wife Salma Carunia for her patience and support as I labored over these pages

Part I: Evolution and the Survivor's Mind

"With me the horrid doubt always arises whether the convictions of man's mind, which have been developed from the mind of the lower animals, are of any value or at all trustworthy."

Charles Darwin

Introduction

Erica Goode, writing in the Science and Health section of the Tuesday, March 14, 2000, issue of *The New York Times*, observed that *A Natural History of Rape* by Randy Thornhill and Craig T. Palmer (The MIT Press Cambridge, Massachusetts, 2000) was not some "fringe theory developed by a pair of renegade researchers," but was instead a piece of a larger theoretical framework known as evolutionary psychology. The discipline, which assumes that the mind is a product of natural selection, seeks commonalties in a species' behavior and, when it find them, argues that they are based on mental structures that evolved, that is on instincts. In the world of the evolutionary psychologist this is true not only of dauber wasps and chaff finches but of human beings as well.

Erica Goode is correct. The critique of rape provided by Randy Thornhill and Craig Palmer is based on – and indeed is an extrapolation of – the thesis that mind, if it exists, must be an attribute of brain function. At one point the authors even sneer at the idea of "an unidentifiable mind distinct from the brain,"[1] and they assure us that "every aspect of every living thing is, by definition, biological, and everything biological is a result of interaction between genes and environmental forces."[2] Since the brain is a physiological component of the body,[3] and since psychological and biological factors are the same,[4] Thornhill and Palmer argue that it is absurd to assume the brain was exempt from the evolutionary forces that shaped the rest of the body.[5] And since the brain is the source of behavior and psychology, those too are shaped by evolution. In the authors' opinion, it is unscientific and even bizarre to believe otherwise.[6]

Quoting George Gaylord Simpson, who in an article "The Biological Nature of Man" published in April, 1966, in *Science* made the claim that all attempts to answer the question "What is man?" before the appearance of Charles Darwin's *Origin of Species* in 1859 are worthless and best ignored completely,[7] Thornhill and Palmer go on to distinguish between proximate and ultimate causes[8] and to cast evolution in the role of an ultimate cause, by which they mean it answers the question "why?".[9] The authors argue explicitly that evolution is a substitute for assuming supernatural explanations (i.e. God)[10] and is itself

sufficient to account for the complexity of living things.[11]   They argue
that natural selection acting on natural variation can, given sufficient
time, account for complex adaptations, though this "takes hundreds or
even thousands of generations."[12]   Such adaptations specifically concern
them and they go to some length to define what an adaptation is and how
it can be recognized.

   "Adaptations," they write, "are traits formed directly by
selective pressures ..."[13] ... mechanisms that ... provided solutions to
environmental problems faced by ancestors ..."[14] ... manifestations of
evolved gene-environmental interactions."[15]   Adaptations, we are told,
"evolved because they helped individuals overcome obstacles to
individual reproductive success."[16]

   Thornhill and Palmer model the brain as a composite "of many
specialized, domain-specific adaptations."[17]   In fact, they root our ability
to behave flexibly in the extreme mental complexity and stability
bequeathed to us by our genes.[18]   However such flexibility is not
infinite.[19] There is indeed a human nature. It is expressed in learning and
decision making,[20] and it has been shaped in the interaction of genetic and
environmental factors.[21] Of course human nature assumes a quality of the
general species that is expressed in a recognizable way in each of its
members. The authors are quite aware of this and note that species can
be distinguished behaviorally.[22] But precisely because such behavior is
flexible, responsive, and to some extent unpredictable, one can infer that
it is conscious.[23] However, beyond a brief and trite discussion of one
functional aspect of consciousness, that it "provides quick adaptive
adjustments of social striving based on the perception of how ... others
view one and helps one build and evaluate alternate scenarios,"[24] they
have nothing to say about it, and their silence is truly extraordinary.

   Now here is the conundrum: genes self-replicating information
storage units.   The information they store has one purpose: to
manufacture protein. DNA makes protein. Indeed, in the early 1960s
Francis Crick, a co-discoverer of DNA, proposed the formula "DNA
makes RNA makes protein" as the "central dogma of genetics."[25] The
authors tell us very specifically that reproductive success is the single
goal that powers natural selection and thus provides the creative
dimension of evolution.[26] However, they also observe that reproductive
success is itself amoral and that to assume otherwise is to commit the
naturalistic fallacy,[27] and they also tell us that we have not evolved to
understand how our behavior reflects the reproductive success of our
forebearers. To understand ourselves, we must study evolutionary

biology.[28] But given such a premise, why assume we have evolved to understand evolutionary biology or any science? Or more fundamentally, since intellectual disciplines like science are aspects of consciousness, how does DNA, which is nothing but a mathematical code for making protein, when shaped by reproductive success generate consciousness?[29]

Our awareness of ourselves as feeling, thinking, identifiable units is absolutely fundamental to what we are, and the basis for the intuition and experience upon which we evaluate everything. And our ability to communicate by using abstractions not only within our species but across species suggests some common experience upon which all consciousness draws. Yet the authors never attempt to explain how a code for making protein and structured by its ability to successful self-replicate could create such an extraordinary reality. They may assert that mind and brain are indistinguishable or that anything that pertains to life is by definition biological, but such assertions and definitions are as ideological as anything Thornhill and Palmer criticize in the social sciences.

Knowledge is based on intuition, and intuition in the world of the evolutionary psychologist, must be based on brain structure, on the ability of the brain to solve specific problems relating to successful reproduction. In other words, the brain of any brain-possessing species is hard-wired to interact with the world in whatever why furthers that end. There is no necessary connection between those brain structures and the world as it really is. The connection is purely functional: solving problems, most of them more or less immediate, that relate to successful reproduction.

There are several points to notice. First, most living things, past and present, have resolved such problems without the benefit of brains. Organisms that specialize, simplify, and reproduce rapidly, flourish. Bacteria, for example, have been referred to as the most successful, and even the most highly evolved, life forms.[30] Second, complex multi-cellular organisms like plants have also solved such problems but have no nervous system. Third, there is no obvious reason to connect nervous tissue with awareness. All that is needed is that a nervous system cause specific effects within specific clusters of cells. Of course we do associate nerves with awareness because we associate them with excitability,[31] but excitability is a function of life itself, not solely of nerve tissue. Fourth, awareness seems to be a quality like mass or holiness. Either it is there or it is not. Once it is there, it may be graded. A thing may be more or less massive, more or less holy, more or less aware, but such qualities seem to be fundamental to certain kinds of existence. For example, relatedness is a reality that has no mass. A quark is a reality that has mass. Sanctity is a reality that has holiness. Secularity is a reality that has none. You and I are realities that have awareness. Iron molecules are realities that do not. Fifth, everything interesting about being alive comes from awareness since without awareness there would be no interest, and it is our interest in being alive that has led ultimately to things like symphonies and science. Those, and not simply protein replication, are the realities that tell us fundamental truths about ourselves.[32]   Sixth, awareness by its nature seems to be unified, and, so far as we know, specific to individual living animals and, if they exist, individual spirits. Finally, the fact that we are aware seems to be fraught with meaning, yet meaning is precisely the kind of reality that falls outside the bounds of Darwinist scenarios.   Of course there are Darwinists who are prepared to assert that this is because evolution proves the universe is devoid of meaning, but such a claim seems self-contradictory since to pronounce the universe meaningless is to make a profoundly meaningful statement about the universe.

The petard upon which evolutionary psychology is hoist bursts in three directions. First, if evolution, or more specifically Darwinism, is true, then evolutionary psychology must also be true. There is no reason to assume that the brain evolved along lines different from any other organ. Second, if Darwinism is true there is no reason why consciousness should have appeared. Indeed, there is no way to account for consciousness. It is as mysterious in Darwinian terms as it is in any other. Third, even if consciousness were a given reality but one shaped by Darwinian evolution, there is no reason to assume it should ever have made something like science possible, and even if it did come up with something like science, there is no reason to assume within the terms of Darwinism itself that the science it invented would be exhaustively true. Therefore the existence of science casts doubt not only Darwinism but the claims of evolutionary psychology itself, and this in two ways. The very existence of disciplines like Darwinism and evolutionary psychology implies that those disciplines are founded upon false premises. Second, those disciplines cannot from within their own presuppositions provide a convincing account of why we should accept them as exhaustive explanations.

This book will be an examination of these problems. In it I will argue that evolution as an explanation of origins is, especially in its

Darwinian version, a defective image we project upon the past, that its defects mean it is as likely to mislead as it is to enlighten, and that if we assume that the universe was created by an entity or entities who remain able to interact creatively with it, evolution is redundant as an explanation and can be rejected (principle of parsimony). I begin with a statement of my thesis. Then in Part One, I discuss the theory of evolution itself, emphasizing the epistemological problem inherent within it. In Part Two I discuss the phenomenon of abstract communication, not only as it relates to human language but as it relates to animal signals in general, and I attempt to show how Darwinism fails from its own limitations to account for the phenomenon. My point in this part of the study is that if Darwinism with all its defects finally fails to account for something as important and widespread as abstract communication, it losses its plausibility and its claims to exclusivity can be rejected.

Endnotes

[1] Thornhill, Randy, and Palmer, Craig T., *A Natural History of Rape*, Chapter 6 "The Social Science Explanation of Rape," section "Metaphysical Assumptions," p. 147   The men insist that any theory employing such a metaphysical assertion cannot be considered scientific (p. 146).   Plainly, however, the real issue, as defined in the quoted passage, lies not in the supposed distinction between mind and brain   After all, both men are quite willing to admit that "when evolutionary psychologists speak of evolved 'psychological mechanisms,' they are actually postulating physiological mechanisms in the nervous system that, at the present stage of scientific knowledge, can only be inferred from patterns of behavior" (Chapter 1 "Rape and Evolutionary Theory," section "Special-Purpose and General-Purpose Adaptations," p 16).   Surely if psychological mechanisms can be inferred, so can mind.   The real issue lies tucked away in the word "unidentifiable"   Obviously what is unidentifiable lies beyond the range of knowledge whether "scientific" or "metaphysical"

[2] Ibid., Chapter 1, section "Biology, Learning, and Ontogeny," p. 20

[3] Ibid , section "Special-Purpose and General-Purpose Adaptations," p. 16

[4] Ibid., Chapter 7 "Law and Punishment," section "'Chemical Castration'," p 165

[5] Ibid , Chapter 1, section "Adaptations Are Functionally Specific," p 15

[6] Ibid , Chapter 2 "The Evolution of Sex Differences," section "Sexual Selection in Humans," p 32, Chapter 5 "Why Have Social Scientists Failed to Darwinize?", section "Threats to Status and to Altruistic Reputation," p 118

[7] Ibid., Chapter 1, section "Evolutionary Theory," p. 3. The Alexander Agassiz Professor of Vertebrate Paleontology at Harvard University, Dr. Simpson argues that humanity's biological nature (by this he means our evolutionary origins) were not appreciated prior to that date and that our evolutionary past must be given primacy if we are to fully comprehend what we are He argues that "nonbiological, nonscientific" approaches, including "metaphysics, theology, [and] art" can still contribute to our self-understanding, but if they fail to take into account that we have evolved from earlier apes, "they are merely fictional fancies and falsities" (p. 473) In his view humanity's three most crucial distinctives are our bipedalism, our ability to use tools to makes tools, and our language which he considers the most diagnostic (p 476) Language, he believes, is involved in our foresight, the characteristic he considers our most important (p 478) He concludes that while we are more than animals, animals we certainly are. One is not quite sure what to make of such dogmatism, especially since our animal status has been generally recognized many thousands of years before the theory of evolution became dominate Nor does Dr Simpson's complete failure to explain how traits like those he lists came to be fashioned by evolution help us understand the importance he attaches to the theory It is true that Darwin believed that his ideas had profound implications for understanding human psychology, but over a hundred years after his seminal work was published, Dr. Simpson, though convinced that Darwin was right, is unable to tell us just what those implications are Nor does he make any attempt to deal with the "fallacy of origins" (the conceit that what a thing is is inextricably bound up in what it was) Apparently contemplating "Whister's Mother" teaches us nothing reliable about humanity unless in the process we muse "well, of course, she evolved "

[8] Ibid., section "Cause Proximate and Ultimate," p 4, section "By-Products of Selection," p 12 - 14

[9] Ibid , section "Cause. Proximate and Ultimate," p 4; section "By-Products of Selection," p 12 - 14section "Natural Selection and Adaptations," p 7

[10] Ibid , Chapter 5, section "Failure to Understand Proximate and Ultimate Levels of Explanation," p. 111

[11] Ibid , section "Summary," p 122

[12] Ibid , Chapter 7 "Law and Punishment," p 153

[3] Ibid., Chapter 1, section "By -Product of Selection," p. 11

[14] Ibid , section "Special-Purpose and General-Purpose Adaptations," p 16

[15] Ibid , section "Biology, Learning, and Ontogeny," p 21

[16] Ibid., Chapter 3 "Why Do Men Rape?," p 53

[17] Ibid , Chapter 1, section "Special-Purpose and General-Purpose Adaptations," p 17

[18] Ibid , p. 18

[19] Ibid., Chapter 6, section "Ideology and the Social Science Explanation," p 152

[20] Ibid , section "Incompatibilities with Evolutionary Theory," p 129

[21] Ibid , Chapter 7, p 153

[22] Ibid , Chapter 1, section "Special-Purpose and General-Purpose Adaptations,' p 19

[23] There is of course far more to consciousness than flexibility Behavior can be compulsive and conscious, and systems can be designed to evidence some flexibility and yet lack consciousness However, as a general rule of thumb, flexible responsive behavior is one key indicator of consciousness, and Thornhill and Palmer in their discussion of its role in social striving admit this.

[24] Thornhill and Palmer, *A Natural History of Rape*, Chapter 1, section "Consciousness,' p 29

[25] Ridley, Matt, *Genome* (HarperCollins, 2000), Chapter 20 "Politics," p 276

[26] Ibid., Chapter 1, section "Natural Selection and Adaptations," pp. 5 - 6

[27] Ibid , section "Natural Selection and Adaptations," pp. 5 - 6, Chapter 12 "Conclusion," section "How can rape be prevented?", p. 199 The naturalistic fallacy is the claim that what is is what ought to be, or that what is exists has moral legitimacy by virtue of its existence. For example, to argue that one's genes predispose one to a particular kind of behavior and that therefore that behavior is morally right is to commit the naturalistic fallacy

[28] Ibid , Chapter 5, section "Failure to Understand Proximate and Ultimate Levels of Explanation," p. 112

[29] Thornhill and Palmer commit two pages to this last question (Chapter 1, section "Consciousness," pp 29 - 30) They assure us that "there is no reason for assuming that consciousness is anything other than an aspect of our evolved biology" (p 29), that it was probably designed for solving social problems (p 29), and that the psychological phenomena surrounding consciousness are based on specific information and on special purpose mechanisms (p 30). One would hardly imagine that consciousness dealt with in such a dismissive way constituted any problem for evolutionary biology at all!

[30] Stephen Gould has made this point   He rejects the idea that evolution embodies principles like progress or "complexification "   The stability of bacteria, he believes, is far more central to understanding the phenomenon of life than is the mutability that gave rise to multi-cellular creatures   He interprets multi-cellular complexity as a pseudo-trend (Stephen Jay Gould, "The Evolution of Life on Earth, *Scientific American*, Vol 127, No 4, October 1994, pp 84 - 91)   See also Matt Ridley (*Genome*, Chapter 1 "Life," pp 20 - 21, Chapter 2 "Species," pp 25, 30) who claims that bacteria can be considered more highly evolved than human beings   It is worth noting that if Ridley's interpretation is correct, it makes a hash of Richard Dawkins' claim in *Unweaving the Rainbow* (Houghton Mifflin Company, Boston, 1998) that, being directly descended from bacteria, each one of us is "a giant megalopolis of bacteria" (Chapter 1· "The Anaesthetic of Familiarity," p 9)   Not so, according to Ridley   We cannot be descendants of bacteria since they are too advanced   You and I, says Ridley, have descended from viruses (Chapter 8 "Self-Interest," p 125)

[31] The words nerve and nervous have the same Latin root *nervus* meaning sinew   Nerve as a synonym for sinew is now rare except in the phrase "to strain every nerve." An excited person was more likely to exhibit strain, to appear sinuous and more alert at the same time. Hence the connection was made

[32] Notice that I am not claiming that such realities are unique to human beings   They are instead particular expressions of communicative awareness   Communication can be found in all kinds
of creatures and even takes place across species   Hence learning based on communication can also be found   It is such learning that is the bedrock of what we call culture. Thus culture may assume a variety of forms in a variety of species. In ours it has assumed such forms as plumbing and traffic laws.

Chapter 1

The Problem of Epistemology and Cosmic Models

Introduction

In 1975 Gunther S. Stent, then professor of Molecular Biology at the University of California at Berkeley, published in *Science* an article in which he argued that (a) the influence of positivism which informed the first centuries of the natural scientific enterprise is waning; that (b) structuralism (of which conceptualism is a type) has become a plausible alternative to positivism; and that (c) the theory of evolution can resolve the dilemma inherent in structuralism's assertion of innate ideas.[1] He then concluded that because the brain has evolved as a survival organ to process information in a particular way, its innate structures are not particularly adept at scientific inquiry insofar as that inquiry attempts to grasp reality on scales much beyond the brain's immediate experience and that certain areas will be forever closed to the scientific method.[2]

While Prof. Stent focused primarily on questions revolving around the human self, I will in this chapter attempt to expand his insight to include all cosmic models   I will argue that such models are not based primarily on objective evidence but instead project the innate substructure of human consciousness. Ludwig Feuerbach in *The Essence of Christianity* (1841) argued that Christian theology is not about God but about human ideals that have been conceived as infinite and projected into the universe via the Hebrew Christ as interpreted by Hellenistic paganism. Thus Christian theology became a means of humanizing an alien universe. In the same way I will argue that cosmic models are themselves not accurate depictions of the universe but humanizations of it.[3] Indeed, as creations of the human mind, they can express nothing beyond sense perceptions manipulated by innate ideas and cultural presuppositions. Thus current scientific models, including models of origin, share more with ancient models,
including models of creation, than they do with any actual events. They are merely the tales we tell ourselves when confronted with that great mystery. They are the way we make an alien universe human.

In the West this problem has been compounded by the classic subject/object dichotomy that creates a fundamental epistemological dilemma. For the rest of this chapter we will explore the origins of that dilemma particularly as those origins related to the emergence of structuralism or conceptualism. This will lay the groundwork for our critique of evolution theory, especially Darwinism, in chapter two, and for our argument in chapter three that evolution, most notably in its Darwinist form, has become thoroughly ideological: the secular creation myth.

Types of Philosophical Questions

Broadly speaking, philosophy deals with three basic types of questions: the ontological, the epistemological, and the axiological. As reflective thought arose in various cultural paradigms across Eurasia, these three kinds of questions were emphasized differently. Around the Yellow River a culture appeared which stressed harmony and emphasized axiological issues. Around the Indus River a pantheistic culture developed which tended to ask ontological questions. Around the eastern Mediterranean and the Tigris and Euphrates Rivers a cultural complex evolved which stressed the distinction between God and creation and as a consequence assumed the ultimate separation of the elements in creation. Epistemological questions tended to dominate in this region. The religious consequences of these differences were profound. Where epistemological approaches to knowledge were paramount, religious expressions tended to stress the cognitive over the ethical or the mystical and to rely on clear and distinct concepts. Where the ontological approach was paramount, religious expressions tended to be intuitive and mystical. Where the axiological approach was paramount, religious expressions tended to stress concrete relationships and ideals like loyalty and harmony. Hence the West has its creeds, India has meditation, and China has Confucianism.

When elements in nature are assumed to be ontologically distinct, the problem of how to attain to certain knowledge about things distinct from oneself becomes critical. For this reason such a distinction encourages epistemological and axiological questions. These questions are not so urgent where pantheism dominates since pantheism posits a common divine identity among all things, an identity that can be experienced at some mystical level. Hence pantheism is far more focused on experiencing truth than on articulating truth. Indeed, pantheists not infrequently assert that truth is ultimately inarticulatable. Epistemological and axiological concerns are secondary concerns among pantheists, so much so that pantheism can be accused of falling into the naturalistic fallacy.

Epistemology could have proved much more significant for the Chinese who had a myth of origins in which the world was created from the slain body of the giant Pan ku, but after Confucius axiological questions with an emphasis on social harmony dominated Chinese philosophy. However, epistemological questions did become paramount around the eastern Mediterranean and the Tigris Euphrates Rivers. While one could conceivably trace the roots of natural science to Babylon, for our purposes it is sufficient to begin with Greece.

The Epistemological Problem

Greek philosophy was born with Thales who lived sometimes between 640 and 546 BC. During the seventh and sixth centuries before Christ, people in the Middle East became very aware of how different their creations stories were from one another, and this awareness began to cast doubt on the veracity of all the stories. Thales for one reasoned that while all the stories could not be true, they could all be false. Furthermore he also recognized that while one of them might be true, it was not immediately possible to determine which one it was. Therefore, he tried to answer the question of origins by seeking evidence in the world itself. His quest was the beginning of what we remember as the Ionian philosophers or the pre-Socratics.

The pre-Socratics founded diverse schools that could agree on very little. It was within this context that Socrates (ca. 469 - 399 BC) was able to lampoon their pretensions so effectively. While Socrates was primarily concerned with axiological issues, his most adept pupil Plato (427 - 347 BC) was engaged with epistemological ones. The philosophy he developed revolved around the question, "How do we know a thing is what it is?"

Recall that eastern Mediterranean cultures, whether influenced by Hebraic or Hellenistic traditions, have generally maintained a distinction between creation and creator. This distinction implies that primordial reality lies outside the observer and hence is obscured rather than illuminated by the subjective. Thus, it needs to be grasped objectively, but the acquisition of objective knowledge under such circumstances is complicated not only by the assumed separation between subject and object, but also by the mutability of both subject and object. We seek invariance in a world characterized by change.

When a thing changes, it becomes different from what it was, yet in some sense it also remains what it was. To become different, yet not completely different, characterizes change. Early Greek attempts to conceptualize change took two basic directions. Parmenides argued that Being, if it changed, would have to change into non-Being. This, he held, was impossible since if Being changed into non-Being it would no longer exist. Indeed, Parmenides argued that non-Being itself could not exist. Thus the world must be full and motion in it impossible. Therefore, Parmenides was forced to conclude that change and even motion itself is illusory. For creatures who come into existence, develop, and die in a world dominated by change and movement, such a conclusion seems unsatisfactory.

Heraclitus, Parmenides' contemporary, argued that change or orderly development was itself the fundamental law of being. Continuous flux was the rule, or, to put it in a more dramatic way, "whirl is king." At first glance, Heraclitus might seem more persuasive than Parmenides, but Heraclitus' position jeopardizes our ability to know anything for sure since what we grasp is, by the time we grasp it, outdate (and, apprehended through our senses, known only in part). On a more basic level, it would seem to reduce change to meaninglessness since it appears to undermine the nature of being After all, we recognize change because there is an underlying subject of change which remains identifiable Yet, if everything changes, then change applies to the underlying subject as well as to the phenomenal world. Thus the identity of the underlying subject is lost and the coherent development which gives change its meaning is forfeited.

Democritus, beginning with the obvious reality of motion but accepting Parmenides' basic argument, concluded that non-Being must exist. However he retained Parmenides' percept that being is indivisible. The visible bodies in the world, Democritus argued, were composed of indivisible units too small to be seen. These units he called atoms. In this way Democritus believed he had solved the dilemma of movement and change by proposing a world in which tiny changeless units of Being moved about in an expanse of non-Being. Plato built upon the solution offered by Democritus, accepting much of his atomism, but, in an effort to explain how knowledge might be possible in such a world, proposing an overlying reality of immutable Forms. Thus in Plato, and in his predecessors, most especially Anaxagoras and Democritus, an idea that was originally theological: that the visible world can be best explained by appealing to an invisible one, was transformed into a basic tool of theoretical science.[4]

The Platonic Solution

Plato, who Karl Popper termed the "the greatest epistemologist of all,"[5] attempted to resolve the Parmenides/Heraclitus dilemma by admitting with Heraclitus the reality of change but denying with Parmenides that it was fundamental. He did this by assuming the reality of Democritus' atoms, but he modified the Democritus model by eliminating the void and substituting instead fluid, an idea that was retained in modern physics in the form of ether until well into the nineteenth century. By positing such a universal fluid, Plato was able to eliminate the paradox of existing non-Being and at the same time account for motion since fluid not only filled spaces between things but allowed for the motion of things within it. However, Plato went beyond this mere synthesis of ideas, significant as that was, and turned his attention to the epistemological dilemma inherent in a model of the world that distinguished the knower from the known.

The true object of knowledge, according to Plato, cannot be this mutable world since our assessment of it is always uncertain. Therefore Plato proposed the existence of a transcendent realm of forms, a reality that was somehow manifested into the chaotic realm of substance to create or express the material world. What we must grasp, Plato argued, is the immutable realm of Ideals or Forms from which our inconstant world derives its ultimate being. Certainty is grounded only in that realm. Whether we imagine it as a realm of universal Forms like Goodness Itself, Beauty Itself, etc., or conceptualize it in terms of mathematics or the laws of reason, it is important to recognize that our estimates of this variable world are rooted in our certainties about the invariable one. Believing that these forms provided the structure or pattern for that which appears to us, Plato also believed that these forms comprised our intellectual framework and that the forms in our minds allowed us to recognize the same forms in nature. Hence his theory of knowledge was based on intuition. Also because the forms posited by Plato were believed to be universal, Plato's theory allowed for the possibility – even the certainty – that arguments having universal validity were possible.

Plato believed that these realms of substance and form were co-eternal with God and that God created by bringing these realms together. Neo-Platonists later argued that the *logos* or rational principle was the agent integrating these realms, a proposition that was to have profound theological consequences.

Plato furthered argued that we know this invariable realm intuitively, that is, our knowledge of it is innate and independent of any method of reasoning. This must be true, he believed, since any judgment presupposes a priori concepts. Such concepts can be made explicit through a process of recollection. This intuitive knowledge is the basis of those generalizations that enable us to comprehend and discuss our world of fluid particulars.

It is helpful to remember that Plato, as he worked to resolve the epistemological dilemma, assumed that time was cyclical and hence that change itself was impermanent. What had been would be again as the future reenacted and became the past. His vision of the cosmos lacked what we would call historical depth. Thus formal reality was structured by recurring temporal patterns in the material world. Change, as he understood it, was real but essentially powerless in a universe of forms and cycles.

Plato's solution, though in many ways unsatisfactory, lay the groundwork for subsequent Western philosophy. Indeed, Plato's influence has been so pervasive that Whitehead famously remarked that all Western philosophy is a footnote to Plato. His comment is obvious hyperbole but captures the point. Because Western philosophers and theologians have generally discriminated between subject and object, they have been confronted with an epistemological dilemma they must resolve before they can address other philosophical issues, and to this end they have tended to embrace Plato's solution or one of its derivatives. In other words, they have assumed either implicitly or explicitly the non-temporal nature of that knowledge which makes possible those generalizations upon which we base communication.

There is some evidence that by the end of his life, Plato may have begun to question the soundness of his own argument (perhaps he was moving toward conceptualism as his later followers like Abelard or Kant did). Nevertheless, Plato's solution to the West's epistemological dilemma was so important that five hundred years ago Calvin called him the most religious of all the philosophers, and earlier in this century Alfred North Whitehead described Plato as standing closer to modern physical science than did Aristotle.[7] His observation is of considerable interest since the Reformation represented a rejection of Aquinas and through him of Aristotle and return to Augustine and through him a return to Plato. Remember that Luther was an Augustinian monk. The Catholic Church for its part remained firmly committed to Aristotle.

Four Types of Causality

While Plato envisioned the realm of forms as transcendent, his most important immediate student Aristotle (384 - 322 BC) imagined them as immanent and future. Aristotle, having embraced Plato's epistemological solution, applied it ontologically to ask, "Why is a thing what it is?" He argued that tendency creates identity. A thing is what it tends to be. In Aristotle's philosophy Plato's formal cause became final cause and teleology was born. Aristotle developed the syllogism to disclose formal tendency. While Plato's thought lends itself to the proposition "I am saved," Aristotle's system tends to support the conclusion "I am being saved." In the distinction between formal and final cause lay one of the fundamental differences between Protestantism and Catholicism.

Through the Greeks the West inherited four theories of causality: material cause, secondary cause (or cause and effect), formal cause, and final cause (or teleology). These four causes defined Western physics and metaphysics until very recently Coupled with this concept of multiple causality was a theological distinction based on the concept of God as creator of the universe (general revelation) and inspirer of Scripture (special revelation). As creator and inspirer God was able to speak to his people through the world he had made and through the Bible. While the church, basing its argument on Romans 1:18 – 22, understand the general revelation as justifying God's reproach of humanity, it of necessity believed that the creation revealed much about God.

By the end of the Middle Ages formal cause was being reinterpreted, first by conceptualists like Abelard (1079 - 1142), then by their followers the nominalists, most importantly William of Occam (birth unknown, death probably around 1349). The conceptualists argued that forms were only mental categories. The nominalists argued that only particular things existed and that what we perceived as categories were nothing more than names we gave to imaginative constructs. While the conceptualists argued that mental categories were innate, nominalists assumed a theory of knowledge which was radically conditioned by culture.

The Rationalists and Innate Ideas

During the seventeenth century the distinction between general and special revelation began to be distorted with general revelation via reason taking precedence over special revelation. Foremost in effecting this change was Francis Bacon (1561 – 1626) who sought to free science from what he understood as the corrupting influence of religion. To this end he proposed two very different kinds of truth: scientific and religious, and argued that the two should remain distinct. Natural philosophers read the book of nature Clergy read the Bible. Next Bacon, by stressing the doctrine of creation over the doctrine of the Fall and judgment, argued that, as God's creation, the world was under the control of God rather than Satan. This bifurcation set the stage for the subsequent conflict between science and religion. Robert Boyle (1627 – 1691) followed Bacon's lead by proposing the model of universe as clock. Isaac Newton (1643 – 1727) who followed was able to use Christian words but with a very different meaning. Instead of traditional Christianity what had been formulated was a new nature religion based on rationalism and empiricism. This transformation was, as John Hutchison has pointed out, accomplished with very little public debate. But as a result by the eighteenth century deism appeared full blown out of the philosophers of the seventeenth.[8] Natural science had been born with a religious twin. It also laid the foundation for a different way of knowing.[9]

We should note, however, that the seventeenth century rationalists who initiated this shift predicated their theory of knowledge on a model of the mind that, like Plato's model, emphasized innate ideas. Among these innate ideas were geometrical concepts, mathematical and logical rules, and ideas of relatedness. Among notions of relation the rationalists included Cause and Effect, Like and Unlike, Whole and Part, Proportion and Analogy, Symmetry and Asymmetry, Equality and Inequality, and so forth. They believed that such innate ideas were fundamental to the mind's ability to objectify existence. That is to say, they attempted to explain human intelligence by focusing on the structure of the mind instead of the general structure of existence itself. However, though they borrowed the concept of innate ideas from Plato, they abandoned the concept of Platonic forms. In this way, by denying that innate ideas had any necessary correspondence to objective reality, they reintroduced the subject/object split Plato, when he proposed the idea of forms, sought to overcome. This meant that, in human theorizing, mental categories took precedence over cosmic structures. Reality, regardless of what it was in itself, had to be objectified in a particular way if we were to be able to grasp it. It had to be conformed to pre-existing models in our minds. In a sense, it had to be humanized. Thus our world models were understood to be fundamentally human models.

<u>The Philosophical Framework of Natural Science</u>

In other words the natural science championed by the rationalists emerged from a specific philosophical milieu. Its emphasis on material and secondary cause completed the attack on formal and final cause. In place of formal and final cause natural science substituted empiricism and measurement, inductive logic, and the quantification of data gathered within a universe presumed to be a continuum closed to outside influences. And these new scientists insisted that their theories, precisely because they were human theories, had to be tested against events in the external world. Thus natural science was held accountable to the unyielding standards of prediction and verification.

Natural science took shape during the sixteenth century and dominated the West into the twentieth. The rise of natural science represented a major paradigm shift that was to have tremendous impact on Christianity. This impact was reflected not only in natural science's emphasis on the universe as a closed continuum, it also made itself felt in its implicit denial of a *logos*.

In the debate between Christians and Neo-Platonists that dominated the Hellenistic world from the second to the fourth centuries, Christian philosophers had reinterpreted the Neo-Platonic *logos* as Jesus. Instead of the rational impersonal principle proposed by the Neo-Platonists, it was Jesus the person who as redeemer, creator, lover, and judge presided over the issues of history and who united the world with God. Jesus the *logos* was secured in Scripture (John 1:1), opened the universe to miracle, and transformed history into a redemptive process. But, operating from the presuppositions of natural science, Jesus the *logos* was increasingly difficult to defend. Universals were reduced to tentative hypotheses based on quantifiable observations. Miracle lost its philosophical justification and was reinterpreted either as a fortuitous natural event or as a symbol of human aspiration. And fate which had informed Greek tragedy and which Jesus overcame was reintroduced as natural law. Natural science offered humans power over nature, but that power was part of a metaphysic that as it was explored was revealed as fundamentally non-human. *Homo sapiens* became a species out of millions that had evolved, a species that would exist temporarily, and which, if in need of salvation, would have to engineer its own.

The intellectual ferment giving rise to natural science was both creative and destructive. It birthed a new paradigm but to do that it needed to slay the old one. Its destructive side expressed what Langdon Gilkey has called a "war with the Greeks."[10] The Hellenistic conception of transcendence which had provided the integrative structure for Christian revelation was its ultimate target. Christian revelation, being based on a series of events in history, required such an interpretive structure to secure it epistemologically. Once that interpretive structure collapsed, as it eventually did under the weight of centuries of concerted attack, the ability of revelation to "speak" with a unified voice was severely compromised. What William of Occam had begun, Immanuel Kant completed. When Kant, in an effort to defend the basis of natural science from the radical skepticism of David Hume, issued his *Critique of Pure Reason* in 1781 North Atlantic culture passed a watershed in its history, and its debate over metaphysical issues would never sound the same.

The Kantian Critique

Immanuel Kant maintained that reason, unassisted by experience, would eventually generate contradictory conclusions.[11] Logic, he argued, is successful only insofar as it is limited to exhibiting and proving formal rules of thought.[12] It teaches nothing with regards to the content of knowledge.[13] The content must be provided by the empirical sciences.[14] But empiricism, or as Kant called it sensuous knowledge, was as manifold incoherent unless structured by reason.[15] To forge coherent knowledge, reason and empiricism had to be employed together, each correcting the other's deficiencies.

Kant understood knowledge as the result of a synthesis of various representations given either a priori or empirically.[16] Since knowledge is not possible without a concept, a general something that could serve as a rule,[17] this general something had to be given a priori.[18]

Kant called this a priori given pure intuition.[19] It was not itself an object, but the formal condition for perceiving an object.[20]

To account for pure intuition Kant introduced the idea of categories. These categories he defined as pure concepts of the understanding, by which he meant that they were given to the mind not empirically but a priori.[21] Kant spent a great deal of his time discussing these categories. For our purposes it is not important to look at them in detail, but we should note the following point. The categories were roughly analogous to Platonic Forms but with this difference: while in Plato's system of knowledge the Forms were universal and made universal knowledge possible, in Kant's system the Categories existed solely in the human mind. There was no way to know for certain if they corresponded to objective reality, but we could know for certain that they corresponded to subjective reality.[22] Thus Kant embraced a type of conceptualism, a philosophical tradition that goes back at least as far as Abelard. The Categories (or pure knowledge) made it possible for the mind to receive representations (or sensuous knowledge).

The faculty in the mind for receiving representations, Kant called sensibility. The effect it produced, he called sensation, and intuitions about the objects of sensation he called empirical intuitions.[23] Discussing sensuous knowledge Kant argued that all intuition was the representation of phenomena.[24] The phenomena themselves cannot exist apart from our knowing them. Hence, we do not know that they are in themselves. We know them only as our mind through our senses constructs them for us.[25] They are sensuous representations only and must not be confused with the object apart from that representation, that is, as the object is in itself.[26] He then argued that intuition and the concepts associated with it are the basis of all our knowledge.[27] Indeed, he believed that the faculty of imposing an a priori unity upon the manifold of given representations was the highest principle of human knowledge.[28] Thus, the synthetic unity of consciousness was the objective condition of all human knowledge and all human thought.[30]

Knowledge of course made judgments possible. Judgments, according to Kant, were generalizations that compassed the many under a single representation. They were expressions of the mind's ability to think in terms of concepts. They made explicit the mind's understanding.[31] Understanding, in Kant's view, was the ability to perceive patterns, categories, and order.

Thus Kant constructed a critical epistemology which, though fundamentally subjective, allowed for the apprehension of objective reality in terms of that very subjectivity.[32] Such a model of truth can be diagrammed this way: **the event itself / the event as perceived / the event as interpreted.** Perception structures the event, making it accessible to the mind, but perception, by structuring the event, also alters it, investing it with the structure of consciousness itself. Thus, according to Kant, the world we see is a fundamentally human world, and therefore a limited one. Other beings might perceive and interpret it rather differently and just as validly.

As long as we are dealing with practical questions, that limitation on our knowledge is of no particular consequence. We learn by trial and error, by tests that produce predictable results. We apply what we learn. We adopt those applications that produce the results we seek. But when we attempt to expand our knowledge from those practical issues to metaphysical ones, when we attempt to answer ultimate questions such as "what is the universe really like?", then those limitations become extremely important because they mean that all we can do is construct a picture of what the universe might look like to a cosmic human limited by the kind of knowledge we possess at any particular moment in history. The principles under which we operate may be quite sound. After all, we use them because they prove serviceable in our daily lives. But the world view we derive from those principles may not be valid because our way of knowing means that we cannot apprehend a thing as it is, we can only apprehend it in human terms.

Let us return for a moment to the concerns articulated by Gunther Stent at the beginning of this chapter. It the brain, as a product of evolution, is a survival organ, how adept is it at solving scientific or philosophical problems? For example, Randy Thornhill and Craig Palmer dismiss as absurd the proposition that natural selection shaped the body but not the brain. The absurdity of the proposition is underlined for them by the fact that the brain controls the body.[33] Indeed, they assure us, it is a physiological component of the body.[34] Thus they argue that to affirm the evolution of the physical while denying the evolution of the behavioral and psychological is scientifically untenable.[35] And, as the body is a composite of many organs, so the brain as imagined by evolutionary psychologists is a composite of many specialized mechanisms.[36] But, they tell us, "we are not evolved to understand that our striving reflects past differences in the reproduction of individuals. Such knowledge can come only from a committed study of evolutionary biology."[37] One wonders why evolutionary biology should have primacy in answering such questions, but leave that aside for the moment. Why should a physiological organ structured solely by natural selection for reproductive success have any particular facility in evolutionary biology or in any other higher level model building enterprise? In other words, as Gunther Stent wondered, if we assume that the brain evolved a series of specialized mechanism that, taken together, helped secure its survival, why assume those mechanisms are particularly good at other unrelated enterprises? Kant would have understood the question immediately.

The Kantian Critique Today

In his Whidden Lectures delivered in January 1975 at McMaster University, Noam Chomsky argued that human knowledge was founded on the mind's "innate capacity to form cognitive structures,"[37] and that such a property could be accounted for in terms of "human biology."[38] The use of the term human biology is significant here since Chomsky suggests that although such structures doubtless evolved, there it is a mistake to believe that some universal capacity for learning unites the various species. Instead he seems to see species has having abilities that are distinct.[40] Of course, as one who accepts evolution, he imagines that complex mental abilities developed over time in the same way that complex organs did [41] Thus he argues, "The human mind is a biologically given system with certain limits and powers."[42] He also notes that there is not evolutionary pressure leading humans to possess minds fitted to abstract theorization and that when human cognitive capacity is well matched to a particular field of inquiry, that is purely accidental.[43] He writes:

> Among the systems that humans have developed in the course of evolution are the science-forming capacity and the capacity to deal intuitively with rather deep properties of the number system As far as we know, these capacities have no selective value, though it is quite possible they developed as part of other systems that did have such value [44]

Thus Chomsky is supposing a kind of Kantian epistemology that, by the very structure which makes human intellectual achievement possible, sets limits on that achievement, and he believes that Darwinism offers a "biological underpinning" for such an epistemology.[45]   He writes:

> [T]here is no reason to suppose that the capacities acquired through evolution fit us to "fathom the world in its deepest scientific aspects."[46]

Nor is he alone in this assessment. Steven Pinker writes:

> Given that the mind is a product of natural selection, it should not have a miraculous ability to commune with all truths, it should have a mere ability to solve problems that are sufficiently similar to the mundane survival challenges of our ancestors   [R]eligion and philosophy are in part the application of mental tools to problems they were not designed to solve [47]

Indeed, he appeals specifically to Noam Chomsky when he writes:

> Maybe philosophical problems are hard .. because *Homo sapiens* lacks the cognitive equipment to solve them [48]   .[T]here are indirect reasons to suspect this is true . .[T]he species' best minds have flung themselves at the puzzles for millennia but have made no progress in solving them. [T]hey have a different character from even the most challenging problems of science [49]

And while Stephen Hawking is critical of Kant's argument that theories about the origin of the universe are self-contradictory,[50] and contends that the reasoning abilities bequeathed to us via evolution should at least prove sufficient to develop "a complete unified theory that will describe everything in the universe,"[51] he is also aware that scientific theories are no more than mathematical models existing only in our minds,[52] and that our sense of time's direction is a psychological phenomenon based in the fact that "we must remember things in the order in which entropy increases."[53] But this twin admission, it seems to me, robs of much of its power Hawking's original reason for dissent. After all, if our sense of time is purely psychological, purely a creation of the way we remember events, then Hawking's thesis that the reasoning abilities we inherited through evolution should be sufficient to develop a theory explaining everything   in   the universe collapses.   If our sense of time is circumscribed by the structure of our psychology, how can we be sure that the same is not also true of our grasp of reason?   Thus how much credit can we assign to those mathematical models that (as he says) exist only in our minds? And with this question the limits imposed by Kant's critique of all such models reemerges as forcefully as ever.

Plainly when Pinker raises the epistemological issue, he applies it to intractable philosophical problems, and when Chomsky discusses the possible limits on what human intelligence can achieve, he refers to specific kinds of problems like in-depth accounts of our normal use of language.[54] After all, both men are evolutionists and would not see evolution because it is "scientific" as falling under the purview of a Kantian critique. Hawking seems more aware of the problem but does not address it adequately.

The problem is this: Kant understood his epistemology to exclude cosmic questions and to invalidate the models we construct when attempting to answer such questions. For example, he writes, "Human reason is by its nature architectonic, and looks upon all knowledge as belonging to a possible system. ... The propositions of the antithesis, however, ...render the completion of any system of knowledge quite impossible."[55] Kant points out that transcendental philosophies assume that reason is qualified to answer those questions that occur to it, but that all such questions to which transcendental philosophy leads are cosmological.[56] He then analyses such questions and concludes that the "*cosmical idea*" which gives rise to them "is either too large or too small for the empirical regressus, and therefore for every possible concept of the understanding."[57] This is the fault not of the empirical regressus but of the cosmological idea itself since it cannot be resolved by an appeal to experience. After all, Kant argues, "It is possible experience alone that can impart reality to our concepts; without this, a concept is only an idea without truth, and without any reference to an object."[58] Kant's purpose, as we noted above, was to defend empirical science against Hume's radical skepticism. To do this he limited the scope of human inquiry to immediate practical problems instead of abstract and ultimate ones. Science had validity as a vehicle for addressing specific issues that could be resolved via direct observation and experimentation. It was not to be a vehicle for building cosmic models for such models would inevitably draw science into the transcendental realm. Evolution of course is a cosmic model.

Conclusion

There are four points I would like to raise based on the above analysis. *First, evolution, particularly in its Darwinian formulation, is a profoundly culturally conditioned concept* The intellectual heritage of the West, the heritage that gave rise to our current cosmic model of origins and development, was born of a dilemma occasioned by the belief that the world was created and that it is distinct from whatever created it. This dilemma was theological. If our ancestors believed that the world was created but was not distinct from whatever created it, the epistemological dilemma would not have arisen. Had they developed a civilization that stressed harmonious relationships over competitive ones, the dilemma, even if latent in the culture, might never have been considered. It follows then that the questions we ask may be based on false premises (after all, the pantheists could be right), or might be consequent to historical accidents that have no enduring significant value. In a few hundred years the debate currently raging over evolution might seem as quaint as the debates that raged over church polity in centuries past, not because the questions were ever resolved but because the intellectual foundations that gave them meaning shifted. In short, evolution is a culturally conditioned theory that attempts to subsume a variety of complex phenomena under the rubric of a single idea, a reality that means it is forever hostage to certain assumptions which may or may not be either true, exhaustive, or enduring.

Second, solutions to the West's epistemological dilemma have always been tentative, yet one's solution will fundamentally effect one's cosmic paradigm The world of the Platonist differs as profoundly from the world of the Aristotelian as the soteriology of the Reformers differs from the soteriology affirmed at Trent, and the world of the conceptualist differs radically from both. Nor do these three possibilities, each with its cosmological consequences, exhaust the alternatives that have been suggested over the centuries. We should also note in this regard that the Platonic or the Aristotelian solution to the epistemological dilemma allows for the creation of credible cosmic models in a way that the conceptualist solution does not. Thus scientifically based cosmic models, whether they are predicated on Newtonian, Einsteinian, or Darwinian assumptions, cannot be true, they can only be tentative.

Third, natural science is hardly philosophically or theologically neutral. Like any intellectual tradition it comes with assumptions that structure its conclusions, that is to say, it has its ideological dimension. The world imagined by the natural scientist is a closed continuum of repeatable, quantifiable events whose possibilities are explicated by material and efficient causality interpreted inductively.[59] The world *as it really is* might well be an opened continuum (or a controlled one) informed by formal and final causality and peppered with unique events, but the practitioner of natural science can, when speaking within his chosen discipline, say nothing of such a world. The limitations of natural science itself enforce his silence.[60]

Fourth, currently within the North Atlantic culture, the epistemological solutions embraced by natural scientists seem to favor the position of the conceptualists, a reality that reveals a profound contradiction at the very core of Darwinism. The conclusions of those involved in the scientific study of learning, language, or general brain functions, integrate most effectively with conceptualist models. Indeed, evolution itself can be understood to underpin a Kantian epistemology, as Stent pointed out. Yet surely this is strange since, as we have sought to demonstrate, a Kantian epistemology undermines the architectonic function of reason that operates in all such models. Thus to affirm a Kantian epistemology should render evolution as a cosmic model unconvincing. After all, the human mind, if the conceptualists are right, is limited by its place in space/time, and by its innate structure that to some degree actually creates that place.   Thus the mind does not experience the would as it actually is but instead experiences a world it pieces together from its own interpretations of its own sensory input. Against the actual world it projects a picture of a world that is fundamentally human in the biological sense of that word.[61] Is there any reason to take seriously the cosmic models imagined by such a mind? It gets worse. The conceptualist who also believes that our noetic faculties are merely the product of a Darwinian process is in a terrible epistemological bind since there is no reason to suppose that a human mind as a mere biological entity is especially well equipped to deal with scientific questions. There is then an exquisite irony at the heart of Darwinism: if Darwinism is true, it should not have been able to produce a mind capable of understanding that Darwinism is true. If Darwinism is false, then the original dilemma of structuralism (how do our innate concepts happen to match so well with our world) reemerges and scientists must cast about another philosophical model to illuminate their work. That so many in the natural sciences are able to simultaneously embrace conceptualism and Darwinism witnesses to the power of Darwinism not as scientific theory but as faith.

Endnotes

[1] That dilemma being, how do those innate ideas happen to match so well with the world in which we find ourselves?

[2] Stent, Gunther S , *Science*, March 21, 1975, Vol 187, No 4181, "Limits to the Scientific Understanding of Man", pp. 1052 - 1057   Structuralism embraces any theory that embodies structural principles   In philosophy structuralism posits the brain as possessing innate structures which, by processing information, make knowledge possible   Conceptualism, of which there are several varieties, is a branch of structuralism that attempts to forge some common ground between nominalism and realism and regards universals as concepts rather than Platonic forms

[3] It does not matter whether one conceives of this humanized projection in biological or cultural terms   In fact, I would argue that from the perspective of materialistic interpretation of evolution the dichotomy between biology and culture is somewhat artificial since cultural constructs merely unpack potentials within biological reality

[4] Popper, Karl R , *Conjectures and Refutations* (Harper & Row, 1965), Part I "Conjectures," Chapter 2 "The Nature of Philosophical Problems and Their Roots in Science," Section ix, p. 89

[5] Ibid , "Introduction On the Sources of Knowledge and Ignorance," section vi, p 9

[6] Calvin, John, *Institutes of the Christian Religion*, Book I, Chapter 5, section 11

[7] Or more accurately Pythagoras as refined and revised by Plato.   See Whitehead's *Science and the Modern World* (The Free Press, New York, 1925), Chapter 2 "Mathematics as an Element in the History of Thought", p. 28

[8] *The Journal of the Evangelical Theological Society* (March 1998, Volume 41, No 1), "The Design Argument in Scientific Discourse Historical - Theological Perspective from the Seventeenth Century" by John C Hutchison, p 100

[9] Timothy Fitzgerald in *The Ideology of Religious Studies* (Oxford University Press, 2000) argues, following Peter Byrne's *Natural Religion and the Nature of Religion* (London Routledge, 1989), that in creating these categories the deists

were involved in a self-conscious ideological exercise by which they hoped both to secure the intellectual foundations of natural science and universalize the Judaeo-Christian concept of monotheism as the basis for all rational religions Thus he sees the categories of "religious" and "secular" as ideological constructs He goes on to argue that the "religious studies industry" has voided the terms of any useful analytical function by applying them too broadly While that may or may not be true, his critique of the terms as used by religious studies scholars is unimportant for us here What is important is the recognition that "the realm of the secular" is an ideological construction intended to serve a specific purpose From this we will argue that secular cosmic models both reveal and are limited by that purpose.

[10] *Christian Theology* (Fortress Press, Philadelphia, 1982), Peter G Hodgson and Robert H King, editors, Chapter 3 "God" by Langdon Gilkey, p. 79

[11] Kant Immanuel, *Critique of Pure Reason*, Preface to the First Edition (1781), p xxiv

[12] Ibid. Preface to the Second Edition (1787), p xxix

[13] Ibid., I. The Elements of Transcendentalism, Second Part Transcendental Logic, sub-part IV Of the Division of Transcendental Logic into Transcendental Analytic and Dialectic, p 50, First Division, Transcendental Analytic, Book I Analytic of Concepts, Chapter One "Method of Discovering all Pure Concepts of the Understanding," Section 3: Of the Pure Concepts of the Understanding, or of the Categories, p. 60, Book II Analytic of Principles, pp 117 - 118

[14] Ibid , Preface to the Second Edition, p xxx, I The Elements of Transcendentalism, First Division, Book I, Chapter 2 "Of the Deduction of Pure Concepts of the Understanding," Section 1. Of the Principles of a Transcendental Deduction in General, p. 79

[15] Ibid , First Division, Transcendental Analytic, Book I: Analytic of Concepts, Chapter One "The Method of Discovering all Pure Concepts of the Understanding," Section 3· Of the Pure Concepts of the Understanding, or of the Categories, p 60

[16] Ibid

[17] Ibid., Book I, Chapter Two "Of the Deduction of the Pure Concepts of the Understanding," Section 2· Of the a priori Grounds for the Possibility of Experience, sub-Section 3: Of the Synthesis of Recognition in Concepts, p 104

[18] Ibid , sub-Section 3 Of the Synthesis of Reproduction in Concepts, p 102

[19] Ibid , I. The Elements of Transcendentalism, First Part: Transcendental Aesthetic, p 22

[20] Ibid., I Elements of Transcendentalism, Book II Analytic of Principles, Chapter 3 "one the Ground of Distinction of all Subjects into Phenomena and Noumena," Appendix: Of the amphiboly of Reflective Concepts, owing to the Confusion of the Empirical with the Transcendental Use of the Understanding, p 219

[21] Ibid , First Division The Transcendental Analytic, Book I, Chapter One Section 3, p 60

[22] The debate as to whether the Categories are universally human, or cultural constructs, or some mixture of both is a debate we need not get into here.

[23] Kant, *Critique of Pure Reason*, I. The Elements of Transcendentalism, First Part Transcendental Aesthetic p 21

[24] Ibid , Part I. The Elements of Transcendentalism, General Observations on Transcendental Aesthetic, pp. 35 - 36

[25] Ibid., p. 36; I. The Elements of Transcendentalism, Book II, Chapter 3, Appendix, p 217

[26] Ibid , First Division Transcendental Analytic, Book I, Chapter 2, Section 2, sub-section 3, p 103

[27] Ibid , Part II Transcendental Logic, Introduction The Idea of Transcendental Logic, p. 44

[28] Ibid , I. The Elements of Transcendentalism First Division, Book I, Chapter Two, Section 1, p 79

[30] Ibid., p. 81

[31] Ibid., Chapter One, Section 1. Of the Logical Use of Understanding in General, pp 54 - 55

[32] It is worth noting here that Popper, though he sharply distinguishes his own "critical rationalism" from Kant's epistemology, claims that, when applied to the philosophy of science, his approach completes the critique Kant began

(*Conjectures and Refutations*, Introduction, section xv, pp. 26 - 27). Kant was correct, Popper believes, when he argued that the human intellect imposes laws upon nature rather than discovering laws of nature, but Kant was wrong, Popper thinks, to believe that the laws humans imposed are necessarily true (Part I "Conjectures," Chapter 1 "Science Conjectures and Refutations," Section v, p 48, Chapter 2, Section x, p. 95). Here, Popper argues, Kant proved too much and that to be glean the truth in Kant's idea, the problem he addressed must be reduced to its proper dimensions Popper believes that instead of asking with Plato "how do we know?", Kant should have asked, "how are successful conjectures possible?". Later Popper affirms in agreement with the idealist that theories are not forced upon us but are human creations, conceptual instruments we design for ourselves to assist us to think about things (Chapter 3 "Three Views Concerning Human Knowledge," Section 6 "The Third View Conjectures, Truth, and Reality," p 117) Thus Popper modifies Kant in the following way believing that Kant's assertion that we impose laws upon nature is too radical, Popper argued that it must be modified to stress that our impositions are free creations of our minds and meet with varying success (Chapter 8 "On the Status of Science and Metaphysics, Section 1 "Kant and the Logic of Experience," p 191)

[33]Thornhill, Randy, and Palmer, Craig T , *A Natural History of Rape*, Chapter 1 "Rape and Evolutionary Theory," section "Adaptations are Functionally Specific," p. 15

[34] Ibid , section "Special-Purpose and General-Purpose Adaptations," p 16

[35] Ibid , Chapter 2 "The Evolution of Sex Differences," section "Sexual Selection in Humans," p. 32; Chapter 5 "Why Have Social Scientists Failed to Darwinize?", section "Threats to Status and to Altruistic Reputation," p. 118

[36] Ibid , Chapter 1, section "Special-Purpose and General-Purpose Adaptations," p. 17; Chapter 5, section "The Naturalistic Fallacy," p 110

[37] Ibid , section "Failure to Understand Proximate and Ultimate levels of Explanation," p 112

[38] Chomsky, Noam, *Reflections on Language* (Pantheon Books, 1975), Part I The Whidden Lectures, Chapter 1 "On Cognitive Capacity," p 23

[39] Ibid., p 32

[40] For example, he points out that white rats are better than college students at learning to negotiate mazes (Part I, Chapter 1, pp 18 - 19 and Part II, Chapter 4

"Problems and Mysteries in the Study of Human Language," pp 158 - 159), a phenomenon that suggest to him that, given the obvious superiority of human intelligence to rat intelligence, there is no general theory of learning that applies to rats as well as humans He also argues that the mental structures enabling humans to learn languages are unique to humans (Part I, Chapter 2 "The Object of Inquiry," p 40), that they are "a species-specific, genetically determined property" (Part I, Chapter 3 "Some General Features of Language," p. 79) Also see Chapter 1, p. 11 for more on language as a species specific property.

[41] Ibid , Chapter 1, p. 10

[42] Ibid Part II, Chapter 4, p 155

[43] Ibid , Part I, Chapter 1, p 25

[44] Ibid , Chapter 2, pp. 58 - 59

[45] Ibid , Chapter 3, pp. 123 - 124

[46] Ibid , p 124

[47] Pinker, Steven, *How the Mind Works* (W W Norton & Company, New York, New York, London), Chapter 8 "The Meaning of Life," p 525

[48] Ibid , p. 561

[49] Ibid , p 562

[50] Hawking, Stephen W , *A Brief History of Time* (Bantam Books, 1988), Chapter 1 "Our Picture of the Universe," pp 7 - 8 He challenges Kant based on Kant's unspoken assumption that time is distinct from the universe and continues backward forever whether or not the universe has existed forever. Hawking agrees with Augustine that the concept of time apart from the universe has no meaning (p 8). He has a point in that Kant does distinguish between space and time, claiming, "Time is the formal condition, *a prior*, of all phenomena whatsoever Space, as the pure form of all external intuition, is a condition, *a priori*, of external phenomena only " (*Critique of Pure Reason*, I Elements of Transcendentalism, First Part, second section, subsection 5 "Transcendental Exposition of the Concept of Time," p. 31) However, in saying this, Hawking implies that Kant thought of space and time as objective realities He did not (see footnote 40)

[51] Ibid , pp 12 - 13

[52] Ibid , Chapter 8 "The Origin and Fate of the Universe," p 139. Hence Hawking concludes there is no distinction between real and imaginary time, a judgment with which Kant would have had no fundamental argument Kant says, "Time.. is the real form of out internal intuition Time therefore has subjective reality   Time is nothing but the form of our own internal intuition   Take away the peculiar condition of our sensibility, and the idea of time vanishes, because it is not inherent in the objects, but in the subject only that perceives them " (*Critique of Pure Reason*, I Elements of Transcendentalism, First Part, second section, subsection 5, p 33)

[53] Ibid., p 147   Such a realization, he notes, means that the Second Law of Thermodynamics is trivial.

[54] Chomsky, Noam, *Reflections on Language*, Part I, Chapter 1, p 25

[55] Kant, Immanuel, *Critique of Pure Reason*, I Elements of Transcendentalism, Second Division· Transcendental Dialectic, Book II On the Dialectical Conclusions of Pure Reason, Chapter 2 "The Antinomy of Pure Reason," Section 3 Of the Interest of Reason in these Conflicts, p 336

[56] Ibid , Section 4: Of the Transcendental Problems of Pure Reason, and the Absolute Necessity of their Solution, p. 338

[57] Ibid., Section 5: Sceptical Representation of the Cosmological Questions in the Four Transcendental Ideas," p. 344 (italics in the original)

[58] Ibid

[59] Notice in this regard that the validity of inductive logic cannot be demonstrated logically and does not derive from experience Yet it seems to be fundamental to the way we process information   Inductive logic may well be made possible by innate structures

[60] Of course a scientist can opine about a preferred cosmic model, but so long as those opinions purport to be scientific, they cannot claim the authority of truth

[61] Darwinists, as we shall see, often describe this mental creation as a virtual world.

Chapter 2

What is the Theory of Evolution?

Evolution as Ordered Change

The word *evolution* means development or ordered change. It comes from the Latin *evolut(us)* meaning *rolled out* or *unfolding* and is etymologically related to the geometric concept *evolute*. As such there is nothing particularly controversial about the term. Development, growth, and ordered change are obvious realities and have been throughout human history. Such concepts rest comfortably within Christian theology which, after all, is predicated on the assumption that God's plan of salvation is unfolding (or evolving) and which emphasizes God's role not only as sustainer but also as continuous creator. The Judeo-Christian doctrine of creation does not require us to believe that God's creative work is done. Indeed, it requires the very opposite of us: we must believe that God's creative work is ongoing. God's role as sustainer is closely related to his role as creator, and God's miracles, particularly his miracles of healing, are examples of immediate creative acts. As Martin Buber, the Jewish religious philosopher observed, in nature God's creative act goes on uninterrupted.[1] In fact, Christians themselves are designated as new creations (II Corinthians 5:17), a reality which inspired the Russian Orthodox theologian Nicolas Berdyaev to christen the Holy Spirit's continuous creativeness in the world "the eighth day of creation."[2]

The Two Illusions

However, as Berdyaev has pointed out, creativity and evolution are mutually exclusive concepts. Evolution is a process controlled by laws whether natural or transcendent while creativity, emerging from freedom, is not answerable to such laws.[3] Creativity, he observes, does not occur by merely redistributing the given elements that constitute the world, and he calls the novelty that appears to result from such a redistribution "pure illusion." Instead he argues that a creative act is not wholly determined by its medium. It arises out of nothing, or out of freedom which is irrational, mysterious, and rooted in nothingness.[4] We should note that though he does not acknowledge it (and may have even been unaware if it), Berdyaev's argument rests on the distinction Aquinas made between creation and change. Change, said Aquinas, before it can occur requires something to be changed. To create, on the other hand, is to cause being itself to exist.[5] The first is a fit topic for the physical sciences, the second lies in the realm of theology. Thus did Aquinas put to bed any debate between evolution and religion a half-a-millennium before Darwin wrote. So why did Darwin's publication *The Origin of Species by Means of Natural Selection* provoke any debate at all, and why does that debate still rage (at least in certain quarters) a century-and-a-half after it was first published?

The question is even more arresting when we realize that many if not most Christians have had no problem incorporating modified versions of Darwin's ideas into their faith expressions, and this was true from the beginning. For example, Asa Gray, a Harvard botanist who maintained his orthodox Congregational witness in the midst of that university's Unitarianism, was an early champion of Darwin's ideas, though unlike Darwin himself, Gray interpreted those ideas theistically. Indeed, Ronald L. Numbers, after conducting an exhaustive survey of the religious professions of the members of the American Academy of Science during the second half of the nineteenth century, concluded that none of the men abandoned his faith because of Darwin's theory. And, he observes, Darwin himself, though he eventually rejected Christianity, did so for theological reasons that had nothing to do with evolution.[6]

However, Charles Hodge of Princeton University was perhaps more prescient when in *What is Darwinism?* (1874) he noted that the real problem lay not with Darwin's rejection of a Creator (Darwin, he observed, "admits a Creator ... explicitly and repeatedly")[7] but in his rejection of design. It is Darwin's use of the word "natural" to assert the appearance of design without recourse to a Designer that is the reason "Materialists almost deify him."[8] When we recall that the appearance of design without recourse to a designer is the very point made by Richard Dawkins in *The Blind Watchmaker*,[9] we see that the debate has never gotten past this point.[10] Dawkins confesses to be so impressed with the evidence from design that had he lived prior to 1859 he could not imagine being an atheist,[11] and he praises Darwin for having made it possible to be an intellectually fulfilled atheist and not just one who defends atheism as logically tenable.[12] Thus while Berdyaev maintains that creation based on the redistribution of existing elements is an illusion, Dawkins points to the appearance of design in the midst of such redistribution and names it an illusion. Both men claim to have disclosed an illusion. Who is right?

To answer this question we should begin by noting that illusions are products of the mind. They are phantoms of the mind that occur when the brain misinterprets sensory data and creates a phenomenal reality at variance with the extrinsic one.[13] In the last chapter we discussed how our perception of the world is created by structures inherent in the brain/mind. In this chapter we will look more closely at the role culture plays.

The Current Culture Milieu

We live in a culture dominated by the idea of evolution. Everything: life, the cosmos, weather systems, personalities, economic and political circumstances, language and culture itself, is said to evolve. Not all cultures have viewed reality in this way. In the past, many cultures, including those which gave rise to our own, conceived the universe and/or its respective parts as static, or else in terms of cycles which masked a basic changelessness. In one sense the older or more traditional view rested on ignorance. Many traditional cultures lacked the perception of historical depth we take for granted. But in another sense the extreme historization we ascribe to everything reflects a profound philosophical shift. In the past concepts like transcendence, necessity, absolutism, generality, and certainty ruled philosophical discourse. Today we think in terms of immanence, contingency, relativism, particularity, and probability. Both sets of terms embody elements of truth and hence may be useful in constructing workable models of reality, but, depending on which set prevails, those models will look fundamentally different. Hence they will explain many of the same things in contrary ways while consigning to mystery phenomena that might seem quite explicable from the other's perspective.

We should note in this regard that a philosophical environment characterized by a nomenclature like relative, contingent, immanent and the like will be much more amenable to evolutionary concepts than will one characterized by a nomenclature like transcendent, necessary, absolute and so on. This can be illustrated by the history of the development of the idea of evolution itself.

Evolution is an ancient concept that in the West can be traced back at least as far as the Greeks, although the Greeks imagined that the extent to which a thing might change was radically circumscribed by its essential nature. Thus, the idea of species as changeless entities also has roots in Greek culture. Either of these notions might have risen to a place of dominance in the West, and both did for different reasons and at different times.

When Darwin published *On the Origin of Species* in 1859, evolution was in the air in western Europe and had been for over a century. As early as the seventeenth century efforts were underway to construct cosmogonies based solely on Newton's principles, and by the eighteenth century European intellectuals were increasingly agreed that the earth and its organisms had changed since they were created, that fossils were remains of creatures that had lived a long time ago, and that matter in motion as interpreted by Newton would be sufficient to explain events in nature.[14] As his life drew to a close even Carolus Linnaeus (1707 - 1778) whose classification system was to prove central to the organization of biology as a discipline and who based that system on the supposed existence of changeless Archetypes, had begun to consider the possibility that species might change and that the Archetypes were not represented by species but by genera.[15]

Jean-Baptiste Lamarck (1744 - 1829) had proposed that species might evolve over time by passing on acquired characteristics from one generation to the next. Georges Cuvier (1769 - 1832), as founder of the twin sciences of comparative anatomy and paleontology, was well aware of how creatures functioned as united organisms and was contemptuous of such ideas, but Etienne Geoffroy Saint-Hilaire, the zoology professor who invited Cuvier to Paris in 1792 and who, along with him, helped to develop the principles of comparative anatomy, found the Linnaean scheme somewhat arbitrary. Its arbitrariness indicated to him that any animal might be transformed into any other. The idea that one species might evolve into another was to him quite feasible. Indeed, in London in the 1820s the physicians and the surgeons of the medical establishment tended as a group preferred the idea of special creation while the more egalitarian general practitioners tended as a group to favor the idea of evolving forms.[16] Ronald Numbers also argues in favor of the premise that liberal religious and political attitudes predisposed one to accept Darwinism,[17] and he notes as well that by 1859 naturalists had generally come to believe that invoking miracles and the will of God was to explain nothing.[18] It was their commitment to "methodological naturalism" rather than rather than the power of Darwin's arguments that brought them over to "organic evolution." *On the Origin of Species*, he concludes, was more catalyst than cause.[19] Thus we can conclude with some confidence that the current prevalence of evolutionary ideas is, at least partly, a cultural phenomenon as we argued in chapter one. As a consequence we might suppose that there are cultural mechanisms at work which will tend to stretch the idea of evolution beyond its appropriate boundaries.

The Components of Biological Evolution

The theory of evolution is based on seven primary ideas, some more controversial than others. They are (1) the idea that, as Genesis puts it, "kind begets after its own kind," that (2) the members of each generation will vary among themselves, that (3) the tendency of each generation is to produce ever greater numbers of its own kind, that (4) limited environmental resources engender competition among individual members of the respective kinds, that (5) environments themselves tend to be unstable, particularly over long periods of time, that (6) this environmental instability encourages divergence among the extant variations of the specific kinds, and that (7) in principle such divergence is for all practical purposes limitless. From evolution so conceived emerges the idea that all life on earth has developed from a common ancestor. But other ideas are also involved. They are the ideas that the way things are is primarily a consequence of chance and that things could have been quite different, that there is no goal, and that material and secondary causality are sufficient to explain all that has occurred.

Let us pause to consider five metaphysical assumptions masked by these assertions: chance, species, survival of the fittest, materialism, and uniformitarianism.

Metaphysical concept 1: Chance

In Ecclesiastes 9:11 we read: "I returned, and saw under the sun, that the race *is* not to the swift, nor the battle to the strong, neither yet bread to the wise, nor yet riches to men of understanding, nor yet favour to men of skill; but time and chance happeneth to them all."[20] The preacher observes that human purpose is canceled by the realities of "time and chance" working in tandem. The Hebrew word translated as chance is *pega'* means that which is caused by accident, that for which one cannot plan because it happens for no known (or knowable) reason(s). Thus chance is a synonym for unpredictability and is in this sense to be distinguished from probability which is a mathematical expression of predictability.   Therefore chance, as opposed to probability, could suggest a universe that is mysterious, without purpose, or both.   The Hebrew people would not have understood the universe to be without purpose, so *pega'* to them meant mysterious as in the ways of God are mysterious but not without purpose.   Currently the idea of chance when interpreted against the background of a godless universe makes   the purposelessness of life immediate.   But from either perspective chance is simply an admission of our ignorance: it reveals our inability to predict. We are the ones who ascribe metaphysical significance to that inability. Chance, depending on one's faith system, may conceal the purposes of God, or reveal a purposeless universe.

Metaphysical concept 2: Species

We began with the assertion that "kind begets after its own kind." Today when we think of kind we usually understand it to mean species.   But what is a species? The word has a variety of definitions, but in biology species derives its meaning from Carolus Linnaeus' system of classification. In that system a species is lower than a genus but higher than a subspecies or variation, and is used to distinguish among members of a genus. We may assume it refers to something objective, that it is not an imaginary construct, but it is worth noting that at the beginning of the twenty-first century no one has come up with a definition of species that covers all cases. The idea of biological species simply cannot be applied inflexibly.   Evolutionists see that as confirmation of evolution.   In a system as fluid as the one proposed by evolutionists, one would expect loose ends.   Daniel Dennett, for example, is inclined to interpret continuing debates over what constitutes a species as a cultural vestige of Aristotelianism.[21]   But among Darwin's original opponents were those who objected to Darwin's thesis precisely because they recognized that his theory undermined the idea of species inherent in Linnaean classification. The Swiss-born American Louis Agassiz, for example, pointed out that Darwinism, since it asserted that species were not fixed but graded into one another, led to a denial of the reality of species, and he argued further that if species were not real, they could not vary. Thus variety in individuals proved nothing about the variability of species.[22]

Hence there was a logical problem with Darwin's thesis. Darwin wanted to explain the origin of a thing by appealing to variation within that thing, but variation within that thing undermined the reality of the thing itself. One could argue then that Darwin was looking in the wrong place. The origin of what he wished to explain lay not in the varieties of the world, but in our own minds. Species are nothing real in themselves but are generalizations we impose, and of course there is no guarantee that our generalizations are accurate representations of reality. Objective reality eludes our abstractions. Scientists who wish to claim William of Occam as a philosophical ancestor should be aware that the above position is nominalism and that William of Occam was a nominalist.

To illustrate, consider homologies within the Linnaean classification. Homologous traits are those which, though sharing similar locations and basic structures in various kinds of creatures, differ in form and function. An example of homology would be the arm of a monkey, the foreleg of a donkey, the wing of a robin, and the flipper of a seal. Charles Darwin published in the middle of the nineteenth century. Carolus Linnaeus was an eighteenth century botanist. He developed his system of classification around homologous structures, understanding them to reflect archetypes in the mind of God. Darwin interpreted homologous structures differently. He saw them as illustrative of the idea of common ancestors. Evolution theory transformed homologies from evidence of archetypes to evidence of descent with modification. Are the two ideas mutually exclusive? If so, which is right? Perhaps it is better to say that archetypes might or might not exist in the mind of God but certainly exist in the minds of people. We might further argue that Linnaeus and Darwin were interpreting the same archetype differently. It would follow then that species is an intellectual construct, adequate in many cases but not truly representative of objective truth. And if this is so, might we not expect members of each generation to vary among themselves as was asserted in point two above? Such variation would prove nothing about evolution, it would be the simple consequence of our imperfect perceptions. (Recall from chapter one that if our perceptions did evolve, we might expect them to be imperfect and hence unreliable guides as we attempt to model a reality mediated across great distances of time and space. This brings us back to the problem that a mind which evolved could in principle say little definitive about the process that created it.) For a further discussion see Appendix at the end of Part I on the problem of classification.

Metaphysical concept 3: Survival of the fittest

The third component of the seven we listed above, that is the tendency of each generation to produce ever greater numbers of its own kind, and the fourth component, the competition for limited resources in a growing population, together give rise to the idea of "survival of the fittest." The phrase was coined not by Darwin but by his contemporary, the English philosopher Herbert Spencer who sought in Darwin's theory a unifying principle of knowledge that could be applied to all phenomena. Ironically, though he insisted he did not deal in metaphysics and other "unknowables," the phrase "survival of the fittest" for which he is most remembered is in fact metaphysical. Notice that the phrase is a disguised tautology. After all, survival reveals the fittest, but survival is precisely what the term fittest sets out to explain. Thus "survival of the fittest" is more accurately "survival of the survivors." So rendered the phrase explains nothing. One might just as meaningfully speak of the reproduction of the reproducers. But this is not to say that the word "fittest" has no function in the phrase. In fact, it expresses a value judgment. Fitness is commonly imagined to involve attributes like competence, like being qualified, like worthiness, like being deserving, and thus, when applied in a Darwinian sense, suggests that those who survive have earned the right because of some "superior" intrinsic merit. Thus "survival of the fittest" celebrates but does not explain. It is a triumphal, metaphysical term and invests Darwinism with a triumphal, metaphysical quality. Little wonder that it was born among, and welcomed so enthusiastically by, the Victorians. Yet this phrase, because it crows so loudly in such convenient shorthand, continues to haunt evolutionist literature, betraying its metaphysical dimension.[23]

Metaphysical concept 4: Materialism

It is not generally appreciated just how metaphysical the concept of materialism is, but notice several things about it.
First, it denies material reality to the spiritual, then attempts on that basis to deny the spiritual any objective validity, but in denying material reality to the spiritual, it makes a metaphysical judgment. Second, it gives primacy to explanations which assert material causes. Third, it is not at all clear what qualities something must have to be declared material. In

the past one might have argued that the material was compassed by the periodic table, but with the coming of sub-atomic physics, such a definition seems inadequate. At the sub-atomic level the material so understood dematerializes and even seems to cease to obey laws that are inviolable at the atomic level. Fourth, materialism is highly interpretative. Not only does it rely on subjective judgments, it structures an investigation around those judgments so as to predetermine its outcome. Data which do not fit within its explicit framework are laid aside as anomalous or explained away. Thus it reduces everything to its own standard. It insists before the investigation has fairly begun that its outcome must conform to the precepts of materialism. All of this means that materialism is a metaphysical concept and serves a philosophical agenda. It is not neutral. It comes with assumptions and consequences.

Metaphysical concept 5: Uniformitarianism

This principle, originally proposed by James Hutton in 1785, is the thesis that geological processes have been the same throughout earth's history. Because the proposed model contrasted so sharply with catastrophism, the one dominate at the time, it was initially rejected until Sir Charles Lyell popularized it during the first half of the nineteenth century. Catastrophism, the idea that periodically cataclysms of various kinds destroyed life on earth and that new ages arose from the rubble these cataclysms left, was generally associated with divine action, of which Noah's flood was the quintessential example. Thus uniformitarianism had immediate and obvious metaphysical implications. However, following Lyell's lead, geologists argued that the evidence from the rocks made more sense when interpreted in light of uniformitarian assumptions than in light of catastrophic ones.

The doctrine has since been expanded to include the idea that all processes have been the same throughout the history of the universe, that the same principles which operated at the beginning of time still operate today and will continue to operate to the end of time. The thesis is based upon the assumed immutability and universality of natural law. Of course our efforts to uncover such laws of nature are based upon our faith that they exist and can be discovered. And if we find later that a law we took to be immutable and universal in fact entertains exceptions, we reject it. Thus the uniformitarianism we assume is faith based and its particular configuration is always provisional. It may also be wrong in particular instances as the current idea that the age of dinosaurs was brought to an end when a giant comet struck the earth illustrates.

We have argued that evolution is a system that incorporates five metaphysical constructs: chance, species, survival of the fittest, materialism, and uniformitarianism.[24] It is easy to see why Karl Popper dismissed evolution as a scientific theory, calling it instead "a metaphysical research programme."[25] A metaphysical research program is precisely what evolution is and as such it differs not at all from other such programs including religious ones.

Now let us return to our discussion of evolution as a theory of biology. Several questions occur. First, is there not a certain tension between the first proposition that kind begets after its own kind and the second proposition that members of each generation will vary among themselves? How much variety will the first proposition allow and still remain true? One may assume proposition one implies certain parameters to variability, but that calls into question proposition seven, that divergence consequent to mutation, competition, and environmental instability is practically unlimited. One may admit proposition seven but insist that its limitless potential is structured, that randomness (the mutations) is limited in its immediate impact and is pruned by environmental factors. Indeed, one may argue, as Richard Dawkins does, that although most of the change that occurs on the molecular level is neutral and therefore effectively random,26[26] natural selection is the very opposite of random.[27] Indeed, he believes that once the process itself begins, the emergence of highly varied, complex, intelligence is inevitable.[28] This is because neutral mutations which by definition are random are not really mutations,[29] (mutations, he tells us a couple of pages later, are not truly random),[30] adaptive improvement by definition cannot be random.[31] Thus one may aver that the limitless potential affirmed by proposition seven is in fact focused teleologically. It is of no small interest that appeals to Darwinian teleology are becoming increasingly common. James Gleick, for example, notes that teleology is a central feature of Darwinian thinking and survives in biology (and science generally) because of Darwin.[32] This would certainly surprise Charles Hodge.[33]

In light of the seven propositions, this appeal to teleology is worth a moment's reflection. How do we explain it? We should note that evolutionists postulate four basic causes or agents to account for evolution. They are selection, mutation, drift, and gene flow.[34] Drift is mere chance variation,[35] and has no adverse affect on reproductive success.[36] Gene flow refers to the movement of genes among populations as individuals move among populations.[37] Mutations are random. Thus the real agent of design is selection, that is the long-term capacity of certain genes to secure reproductive success. Thus selection, as evolutionists stress, is not a random process. However, nonrandomness of itself does not translate into teleology. I suggest that when evolutionists appeal to teleology they do so because of the incredible claims made in the name of evolution itself, particularly the claims that all living creatures from prokaryotes to Persian cats developed from a single organism that arose somewhere (perhaps even in interplanetary space) once,[38] and that mutation and natural selection are sufficient to explain the appearance of consciousness, communication, culture and the like. Can mutations coupled with natural selection carry the weight? As mathematician David Berlinski asked with such telling effect in the "Firing Line" debate on evolution conducted at Seton Hall University in South Orange, New Jersey, and aired by PBS on Friday, December 19, 1997, how many changes does it take to turn a dog-like mammal into a sea-going whale?[39] Let us consider that specific question for a moment.

According to evolutionists, the transformation that accomplished this feat took place during the Eocene between fifty-five and thirty-four million years ago.[40] Based in large measure on studies of how mammals swim conducted by a zoologist with the happy name of Frank Fish who works at West Chester University in Pennsylvania, and fossil finds in Pakistan made by Phil Gingerich of the University of Michigan and Hans Thewissen of Northeastern Ohio University's College of Medicine, the following provisional scenario has been proposed: whales evolved from mesonychids (a vaguely defined category of mammals that varied from the rat sized *Haplodectes* to the gigantic *Andrewsarchus*) over a period of twenty million years. During that time, creatures moved from a dog paddle to an otter-like kick-and-thrust which was eventually refined into the fluke enhanced undulation of a modern whale. In the course of these modifications whale progenitors lost their fur and their hind legs while their subcutaneous fat was transformed into blubber to help insulate the now furless creatures and to give them buoyancy, and their tails grew massive with muscle, took over half their body length, developed a spherical vertebra that would enable it to bend sharply, generating significantly greater thrust, and spread into flukes. Creatures like

Pakicetus, a furry mesonychid that dog paddled, *Ambulocetus*, Thewissen's "walking whale" which probably behaved much like an otter, and *Rhodocetus* which, though it could swim like a whale still had the seal-like ability to creep ashore, are imagined as intermediate steps. The suffix *cetus* in each of the names identifies the animal as part of the whale lineage.[41] Then sometime between 43 and 40 million years ago the first species of whale arose that were entirely aquatic.[42]

Zimmer notes that this tentative phylogeny of whales is based on reconstructions of very limited fossil remains and that molecular studies do not confirm all the details. He also notes that the relationships among mesonychids are very unclear, that some types which appear more primitive are in fact dated later than some times which appear more modern, and that whales may share a common ancestry that is even more recent.[43] Of course, should that prove true, it would mean that these phenomenal changes would have taken place in even less time.[44] As to how many specific changes this took, no one seems to know. And remember that these changes would not have been tacked on randomly, they would have to have been integrated into a single functioning system to form a successful organism. Thus any mutation that moved the animal along from dog-like to whale-like would have resulted, either directly or indirectly, in a host of related physical alterations. Remember too that DNA is a very stable molecule and would have had to accomplish all this solely through the synthesis of protein.

Dawkins and other convinced evolutionists believe that errors in DNA copying are sufficient to account for such variety. As representative of the group, Dawkins argues that the cumulative effect of tiny changes is a powerful idea and can explain what is otherwise inexplicable.[45] Charles Darwin apparently had his doubts and thought domestic dogs were descendants of several wild species because he found it hard to believe that so many varieties could have derived from one.[46]

Evolution theory does entail some extraordinary propositions. Consider deoxyribonucleic acid or DNA. This long molecule, a double helix built around a chine of alternating deoxyribose and phosphate subunits linked by four bases: adenine, cytosine, guanine and thymine,[47] has only one function: it assembles protein from amino acid sequences. That means that the vast variety of life confronting us expresses nothing else but variations in amino acid sequences. The visible characteristics of any organism are the end results of a complex interplay between the environment and the amino acid sequences produced by genes. At the genetic level there are no brown eyes, there is no aptitude, no wavy hair. There are only proteins.

DNA is an extremely stable molecule. The spontaneous mutation rate for genes is about one in one hundred thousand per generation, while for each base pair in a DNA molecule it is about in one in one hundred million per generation. When mutations do occur, their influence on the phenotype is usually slight, and overwhelmingly likely to be detrimental. Those that are beneficial may exert their influence in very indirect ways. One gene might regulate the effects of a protein made by another gene. Some genes work best in cooperation with dozens of others. After all, organisms are complex with many interrelated functions and a change in one function may well necessitate changes in a host of others. Furthermore, while mutations might accrue in somatic cells over the course of a life, only mutations that appear in sex cells are significant for evolution for only those are transferred from one generation to the next. One need not be a country rube to wonder if mutations have the power to generate the tremendous variety of life we see around us, or to doubt that all that variety derived from a single ancestor. Indeed, I suggest the evolutionists' appeal to inevitability underlines the reasonableness of a skeptical response when one is confronted with such claims.

Earlier in this chapter we suggested that the cultural milieu might have created an environment in which the idea of evolution might be pushed beyond its appropriate boundaries. I suggest that the reappearance of appeals to teleology is an indication that this has happened. But before we proceed further, it is appropriate to pause and consider just what appropriate boundaries for evolution might be. If evolution is a science, then the its boundaries should be established by science. There are two parts to this proposition. We will look at them both.

The boundaries of science

Any field of inquiry is limited by its basic character. What is the character of science and what are its limits? As we argued in the last chapter, science is a field of inquiry based on empiricism and inductive logic. Such a regime addresses the universe as though it were a closed continuum of repeatable, quantifiable events whose possibilities are explicated by material and efficient causality. Of course such an approach might not model the universe as it actually is. The most one who uses such an approach can say is that it generates certain kinds of answers that may be more or less convincing to those who adopt the approach. As Karl Popper observed: an hypothesis cannot be proved, only corroborated.[48]   Thus, a scientific hypothesis must always remain tentative.[49]   Indeed, Popper thought that a hallmark of bad science was its desire to be right.[50]

Using the insights of neurobiology which show us a brain closely integrated with our imperfect senses and structured in such a way as to filter and interpret data derived from those senses, and adopting conceptualism or structuralism as the philosophical traditions that seem best equipped to take advantage of these scientific insights, I think we can further modify and constrain the province of science. I argue that the philosophical limitations of science coupled with the intellectual limitations of humans render futile our efforts to arrive at comprehensive explanations.   The reality is not that science will never provide conclusive answers to questions like *Who am I? Where did I come from? What is my purpose? What is my destiny? What does it all mean?*[51] It will not, but there is nothing particular striking about such a conclusion. The reality instead is that through scientific study we can never arrive at complete general explanations.   It would follow from this that the limitations of science reduce to imaginative exercises scientific attempts to develop cosmic models, and that the persuasive powers of those models are purely system dependent.   They are at best research paradigms. Thus they must be considered to be forever provisional. To take them as more than provisional is to absolutize them and create faith systems of them.

If this hypothesis is correct, we might expect many of our classifications to admit exceptions.   We might except cosmogonic theories to be freighted with philosophical conundrums, and we might expect the models we develop based on such cosmogonic theories to be forever incomplete.   Give such a thesis, how does evolution fare as science?

Evolution as science

Western history is littered with rejected paradigms: the mythic paradigm of traditional societies, the substance/form paradigm of the Greeks, and the clockwork paradigm of rationalist cosmology, each had its day and was abandoned in favor of the organic/process paradigm that currently dominates. Ptolemy and Newton proposed models of the universe that were predictive, persuasive, and to a significant degree empirically verifiable. Nevertheless both of those models have been discarded, Newton's after a much shorter reign that Ptolemy's. The same thing is now happening to Einstein. As is well known the model of the universe projected by the theory of general relativity and the one projected by quantum mechanics are incompatible. If one is right, the other must be wrong. Today the weight of the evidence seems to suggest that the theory of general relativity will have to give way. It simply does not hold up in the subatomic realm where quantum mechanics is supreme. Yet in terms of generating inferences that can be tested and verified, both theories are among the most successful ever proposed. In the study of heredity Lamarck, though he enjoyed a brief renaissance in the Soviet Union, has been supersede by Mendel. In geology catastrophism has been replaced by uniformitarianism, and now uniformitarianism is giving way to a modified version of catastrophism. Nor is science the only field of endeavor to have its occasional revolutions. Human beings often change their ways of thinking, and sometimes these changes are global. Authoritarianism has gradually ceded power to democracies, planned economies have been overthrown by free markets, the gods of Africa are bowing to Christ while the gods of Europe who bowed to Christ centuries ago have revolted and are furtively seeking their old thrones. So it should surprise no one if evolution theory is discarded for another idea.

So why the acrimony over evolution? It cannot be because evolution is, as is so often claimed, the great integrative principle of contemporary biology so that to attack evolution is to attack biology. In fact one can make a case that Linnaean taxonomy is biology's great organizing principle and is more fundamental to the discipline than evolution. After all, if evolution were abandoned, Linnaeus would still remain, he would simply be interpreted differently. Besides, as we pointed out above, the idea that species evolve creates problems for Linnaean classification.[52] So it cannot be that evolution is integral to contemporary biology. But even if it were, so what? Is contemporary biology such a fragile plant that it cannot stand the jolt of new ideas? Must intellectual progress or truth itself be held hostage to contemporary biology? Besides, even if evolution were the great integrative principle of biology, why should biologists care if non-biologists reject the idea? Yet plainly biologists care deeply, so much so that their writing can become quite florid when the subject is broached, so much so that they have been less than candid about weaknesses in the theory as we shall see in the next chapter.

The acrimony over evolution theory cannot be the result of hostility toward science. Science reaches so deeply into our culture that it is well neigh impossible to be hostile to it per se. Besides, many of those most critical of evolution have not been notably antagonistic to science generally[53] while many who have been noticeably hostile to science embrace evolution as an integrative principle justifying their world view.[54] So the acrimony toward evolution cannot be the expression of some deep-seated antipathy toward science.

The acrimony over evolution cannot be the result of a cultural suspicious of new ideas. The theory in its modern form has been around for almost two hundred years. And Darwin never claimed to be original. He merely adopted and reworked ideas that had been floating through Western culture for many centuries before that. Besides, other theories more radical have been embraced with enthusiasm by the very people who vigorously reject evolution. Einstein was a genuine revolutionary. The concepts of Absolute time and Absolute rest that had been foundational to science's concept of the universe at the very moment in history when physicists believed they were on the verge of solving all nature's riddles fell before his relentless equations, yet there was hardly a demure. Instead Einstein became a folk hero. One cannot argue that this is because those who idolized him were not impacted by his work. The atom bomb, which flowed directly from his achievement, has had a much more immediate impact on people's lives than anything Darwin did. It is worth pointing out in this regard that Darwin, who had taken his Bachelor of Arts at Cambridge where he had not shown himself a very diligent student, was a trained Christian minister.[55] Einstein, who had been educated at the University of Zurich where he studied physics and showed his brilliance early, was a Jew at a time when anti-Semitism was far more widespread than it is today. More strikingly he was a Jew whose ideas of God borrowed much more from the pantheism of Spinoza than they did from the God of Abraham, Isaac, and Jacob. Yet Darwin has been reviled while Einstein was feted.

I think instead that evolution has generated such antipathy because of a philosophical bias in our culture that has stretched the idea beyond what is appropriate for it based upon its premises, beyond what the science buried within the concept will bear. In its present form evolution argues that Earth is very old and that the universe is much older. Current estimates put the age of the earth at some four-and-a-half to five billion years, the age of the universe at some fifteen to twenty billion years. Next it argues that life, interpreted as chemistry, originated spontaneously from an interplay of events fairly early in Earth's history, sometime earlier than three-and-a-half billion years ago.[56] This threshold had to be reached only once. From this single replicating living molecule, a process was initiated that would either inevitably, or randomly, or both, produce all the life forms that exist or have every existed. This process was fueled by genetic mutations occurring in a molecule that almost never mutates. Most of the mutations when they did occur would have been detrimental, that is to say, they would have been eliminated by a process called natural selection. Natural selection then works with the stability of DNA to limit variety. By far the vast majority of the life forms originating through such a process, probably well over ninety percent of them, are extinct. Of the survivors, many have for obscure reasons endured for tens or even hundreds of millions of years unchanged, while others have for equally obscure reasons produced a plethora of forms. All creatures living today including human beings are a result of this process. That is, I think, a fairly accurate, if brief, view of what evolution is. What scientific evidence undergirds it?

In asking this question we need to distinguish between *microevolution* which is small scale variation over relatively short periods of time, and *macroevolution* which is large scale variation over much longer periods of time. No one seriously disputes that microevolution occurs. It can be observed, and the mechanism underlying it is well understood. Breeds of cattle are examples of it. Macroevolution, however, does create dispute of two different kinds. First, one may doubt that it occurs, and dismiss much of the data produced as evidence for it as so highly interpretative to be very unpersuasive. For example, it is an empirical fact that humans and chimpanzees share many morphological and genetic similarities. Linnaeus, who grouped species together based on their similarities, was the first to link humans to apes, monkeys, and lemurs,[57] classifying them under the order Primates. However, Linnaeus did not interpret those similarities as evidence of common ancestry, seeing them instead as evidence of Archetypes. If humans and chimpanzees shared a common ancestor, that would be an example macroevolution. But of course nothing like that has ever been observed, or could be given the periods of time allegedly involved. And the evidence cited in support of the idea that the similarities between the two groups shows they share a common ancestry is system dependent and circumstantial.

The hypothesis that humans and chimpanzees diverged from a common ancestor no more than five million years ago would be one interpretation of evidence within the framework of macroevolution. Such interpretations may create controversy within such a framework without in any way jeopardizing that basic framework, and this brings us to the second kind of dispute engendered by macroevolution: one may question how it occurs. Few biologists today deny the reality of macroevolution, believing it to be a well established phenomenon, but there is much disagreement over mechanism(s) behind it. Some like William Bateson (1861 - 1926), the English biologist who coined the word "genetics," and his disciple Richard Goldschmidt who in the 1930s coined the phrase "hopeful monsters," argue that radical variation between one generation and the next is the actual power behind macroevolution. Others like Richard Dawkins insist that given enough time small changes will do the job. Still others are moving toward a synthesis of these two views, arguing that whereas small changes in isolated environments probably do most of the heavy lifting in evolution they may be aided occasionally by a boost from a hopeful monster.

We should pause here a moment to consider the place of species in all this. The term, as we indicated above, is a rather fluid one. Nor is there anything novel in recognizing this. Linnaeus himself had, by the end of his life, begun to wonder if species might under some circumstances give rise to other species, that perhaps genera rather than species was archetypal.[58] Darwin, when he published in 1859, was writing about the origin of species. He acknowledged a Creator but doubted that all the extant species were shaped directly by that Creator. They might, Darwin reasoned, have been the result of the interplay of natural forces, that life might have been invested with sufficient plasticity to adapt itself to various environments without the necessity of divine intervention at every turn. In this he was not so far removed from the later Linnaeus.[59]   But Darwin differed from Linnaeus here: he also imagined that all of life might be interconnected in just this way, that there were no Archetypes, or if there were, they were few and far removed from the plethora of forms alive today. Therefore we should ask where in the division between microevolution and macroevolution do species lie.   If a species developed, would that be an example of microevolution or macroevolution? The question is further complicated when we realize that varieties of living forms might develop species in different ways. Biologists today classify living forms into five kingdoms: Animalia, Planyae, Fungi, Protista, and Monera.[60] Initially species were demarcated based on the ability of matings to produce fertile offspring, but this assumes sexual reproduction, and not all the representatives of the five kingdoms reproduce sexually. For example, it sometimes happens that chromosomes will divide but the nucleus will not. This chromosome doubling is called *polyploidy* and, though very rare in animals, is fairly common in plants. Many of the plants we cultivate are polyploids. When polyploidy occurs, a new species is created instantly. It is not easy to see how this would be an example of macroevolution. Therefore in the division between micro- and macroevolution, it might be safest to categorize the development of new species as an example of microevolution.

We noted above that the evidence in support of macroevolution is system dependent and circumstantial. It is now time to look at some of that evidence. What are evolution scenarios? How are they constructed? What is their significance?

There are two kinds of evolution scenarios. The first expresses an attempt to construct a picture of what must have occurred in ancient times based on the evaluation of evidence. The construction of such scenarios has much in common with history and reminds us that science was originally called natural history. The second kind of scenario is termed a "Just So" story. Such stories are not intended as actual descriptions of what may have occurred. Instead they have an apologetic function. They are trotted out in response to objections based on the argument that evolution could not possibly have produced this or that feature. Their importance to evolutionists lies here: Darwin proposed three tests that could prove his theory wrong. One of those tests was the existence of a complex organ that could not possibly have developed from the accumulation of numerous slight modifications. Critics of Darwin often challenge his theory at this point by saying they cannot imagine how a particular feature could have evolved. "Just so" stories are the evolutionist's rejoinder. If the critic claims to be unable to imagine something, the defender will imagine it for him. These exercises in imagination are intended to answer what Dawkins has called "the argument from personal incredulity."[61] We should note however that such illustrations are system dependent. Hence their seductiveness rests largely on the personal credulity of those who make them or find them convincing. Indeed, as we noted above, the improbability of these "Just So" stories is underlined by the appeal to inevitability to which Dawkins and others have retreated. As Pat Shipman has pointed out, what a particular scientist can or cannot imagine does not constitute evidence.[62] Evidence and argument are different things. For example, discussing the purpose and origin of feathers, Shipman claims to be able to easily imagine how down might evolve as pennaceous feathers degenerated.[63] By the next page this act of imagination is transformed into an argument that pennaceous feathers evolved apart from any thermoregulatory need. But Shipman concludes the evidence under girding the thesis is ambiguous. An argument, she notes, may be rational but lack confirmation.[64] She also points out that in constructing evolution scenarios, the fossil record must have preeminence. All kinds of things might have happened, but only fossils can document what actually did.[65] Her observations are germane to our investigation into the scientific status of evolution. The reasonableness of scenarios often masks the paucity of real corroborative data. Plausibility is not proof.

We will begin our analysis of these scenarios by looking at an interpretive principle commonly used in constructing them: the principle of parsimony or, to give it another name, Occam's Razor. William of Occam was a Franciscan and a scholastic philosopher who embraced a position called nominalism. According to nominalism, reality lies only in individual things. Universals are simply abstract signs we give to these individual things. The maxim of Occam's Razor, that assumptions used to explain a thing must not be multiplied beyond necessity, is intimately tied up with this view of reality. The principle of parsimony, that the simplest explanation consistent with the know fact is the best, is a variation on Occam's proposition. Notice, however, how this principle might be applied given two different models of the universe. In a model that assumes a closed continuum of material and secondary cause, an appeal to God would be a violation of Occam's Razor. In a model that assumes an opened or a controlled continuum, an appeal to other causes would be a violation of Occam's Razor. Thus parsimony functions to make explicit what is implicit in the world model one has already adopted. It has no other role to play. Notice as well that it might not be true, and given certain models, it might not be especially useful. For example, if a chaos paradigm is adopted, then unstable initial conditions could embrace so many elements generating so many effects of so many different sorts that parsimony would soon be swallowed up in opulent extravagance. Thus Occam's Razor precisely because it is an interpretive tool, predisposes one to draw certain conclusions, but they are not necessarily conclusions that accurately model our baroque reality.[66]

Let us look next at fossils. The existence of fossils is often adduced as proof of evolution. In fact, they are proof of nothing. They simply exist. We try to explain them by interpreting them. How might they have formed? What do they signify? And so forth. If we interpret them as artifacts of the Devil scattered around to fool us, we will draw one set of conclusions. If we imagine they are the preliminary sketches made by a creator or creators who were working out the details of the world they wanted to build, we will draw another set of conclusions. If we think of them as the mineralized remains of earlier life forms, we will draw still another set of conclusions. But the fossils exist however we try to explain them. Thus fossils do not prove the theory of evolution. The theory of evolution is instead a way of explaining fossils.

Now one might argue that while fossils themselves are neutral as proof, they do become significant when their arrangement is taken into account, that is, if evolution as we described it above is true, one might expect that older fossils would be more "primitive" and younger fossils would be more "advanced," and that certain connections between earlier and later fossil forms might be evident. On balance this seems to be true, but it does not prove evolution any more than it proves biblical creation accounts. It is interesting to note that biblical creationists have been no less innovative in reading the creation week into the fossil record than evolutionists have at reading evolution theory into it.[67] The fossils are there. The patterns are imposed.[68]

For example, consider the story of the Devonian drought, how it disappeared into a fetid swamp, and how evolution scenarios evolved in tandem with this transformation. In the early twentieth century, the paleontologist Alfred Sherwood Romer advanced a theory of the evolution of tetrapods based on a paper by the geologist Joseph Barrell in which Barrell argued that the Old Red Sandstone Formation which characterized the Devonian was evidence that the period was a semi-arid time of frequent droughts. Romer hypothesized that frequent droughts over a prolonged period (the Devonian covered approximately fifty million years) could have created conditions that encouraged lobe-fin fish to evolve appendages that would enable them to crawl from one dwindling and over-crowded pool to the next. He noted that all known examples of lungfish live in fresh water, and that fresh water ponds would be the ones affected. Thus Romer argued adaptations to life in the water might prepare an animal for life on land, thus easing the drastic nature of the move across environments so radically different from one another.[69] The trouble was that the desiccated Devonian turned out to be an illusion. The more paleontologists dug through the Devonian strata, the more convinced they became that the period, rather than being semi-arid, was lush with fern and forest. Worse, the earliest lobe-fins turned out to be marine fish who developed their peculiar adaptations while still in the deep sea. (The famous coelacanth first caught in the Indian Ocean in 1938 is an example.)[70]   Of course it did not take evolutionists long to come up with a matching scenario. In the new abstract lobe-fins did not creep from one dying pond to the next gasping heated air through nascent lungs. Instead they dashed about through miry coastal wetlands where water, drained of oxygen by sudden bacteria blooms, proved periodically incapable of sustaining the lobe-fins and created an environment in which those that developed lungs had an advantage.[71] Strangely the small fish on which the lobe-fins fed did not respond in a similar way to such evolutionary pressure and seemed to thrive, but such are the fortunes of random evolution.

Of course there is nothing wrong with changing one's theory to fit the facts. But notice that either theory might be correct. Fifty million years is a long time and could embrace a lot of droughts that might well have occurred repeatedly in isolated areas, and these droughts may have given the final push in transforming lobe-fin to tetrapod, so Romer's synopsis could still be true. On the other hand, the alternative looks quite plausible given the new evidence. So the new evidence, though it substantially changed our view of what the Devonian was like, did not eliminate a theory but allowed for the creation of a viable alternative. We now have two plausible stories to account for a phenomena. In time we may end up with two more. Imagination patterns the details. Evolution is the story we tell ourselves as we contemplate those patterns. What is really being said is this: our model of the universe leads us to believe that lobe-fins were transformed into tetrapods some time between four hundred and three hundred and fifty million years ago but we don't know why.

Notice though that we pretend to know how. What does not vary in either of these scenarios is the underlying mechanism: small changes accumulating over time under pressure by natural selection created the panting fish that hobbled from puddle to lake, as well as the sprinters that sucked air above fetid bacteria-choked water filled with darting minnows. That after all is what evolution is. The content of the stories is quite irrelevant. If mesonychids could produce the bottle-nosed dolphin and the blue whale, if raptors could give rise to wrens, if a squirrel-sized Eosimias leaping about in the forests of southern Asia forty million years ago could be the well-spring of gorillas, lemurs, and Mars probes, then the particular story matters little. What counts is that all this was brought about in a random way by an accumulation of small changes over vast periods. The eighteenth century flourishes.

Evolution scenarios as parables

A parable is a story that uses comparison or analogy to convey some meaning in an indirect way. Notice how the alternative stories crafted to illustrate the course of evolution act as parables. Their plasticity suggests that the details (which against the backdrop of tens of millions of years are breathtakingly meager) are not terribly important. But the appeal to teleology, as well as the anthropomorphism in which the descriptions are often couched, suggests the stories have a plot, and that there is a principle enshrined in that plot. The plot is to account for the present solely in terms of the past. The principle is that change itself is creative.

Recall our earlier distinction between change and creativity. That distinction, going back to Aquinas and through Aquinas to Aristotle, rests on the assumption that creativity brings something new into existence while change works to reshape what already exists. In evolution that assumption is implicitly denied and the distinction is lost. Existence is the brute fact emerging from some cosmic "singularity" eighteen billion or so years ago. It is something for which we cannot account and perhaps need not account. It just is, and as such becomes the philosophical equivalent of uncreated matter posited in Antoine Laurent Lavoisier's "law of conservation of mass."[72] But mutations (from Latin meaning "a changing") operating on this extant matter generates novelty or at the very least unlocks the potential of what exists. Unlocking the potential is a way of factoring in teleology but this must not be understood to mean that there is one predetermined outcome. The evolutionist would argue that there are many potential outcomes embodying many teleologies (randomness requires this which is why chaos theory as appeared to evolutionists as a godsend). Two points ensue. First change is creative. Second, evolution is descriptive or retrodictive rather than predictive. As Zimmer says, it may look obvious in hindsight but its future cannot be known.[73] It follows from this that as a theory macroevolution cannot be tested in the way traditional science can be tested. It is nothing other than a system dependent description of the world. At best it can only say: given these assumptions the universe when looked at in a particular way appears to be thus and so. Scenarios of events in the ancient world are parables to illustrate that perspective. In fact they differ little from "Just So" stories.

It is precisely here where the contemporary cultural milieu with its emphasis on immanence, contingency, relativism, particularity, and probability serves to stretch microevolution into macroevolution. In the process evolution scenarios imitate traditional experiments and lure scientists into areas that are far beyond the established boundaries of science. In such a milieu evolution theorists seize on metaphysical concepts like chance, species, and survival of the fittest to smooth over tensions that exist among the basic propositions upon which they wish to build. At the same time they appeal to teleology and "Just So" stories to act as apologetic devices in an effort to mask the improbably of what they propose. Thus macroevolution like so much quasi-science becomes captive to a dozen agendas and is drawn into the public arena in such a way as to tempt scientists to dissimulate concerning their own doubts not only about the divergence proposals comprehend by macroevolution but about its very status as science as we shall see in the next chapter.

Endnotes

[1] *Four Existentialist Theologians*, edited by Will Herberg (Doubleday & Company, Garden City, New York, 1958), section on Martin Buber, essay "Dialogue Between Heaven and Earth," part iv, p. 200

[2] *Ibid.*, section on Nicolas Berdyaev, essay "Religion of the Spirit," p. 113

[3] Berdyaev, Nicolas, *Dream and Reality* (The Macmillan Company, New York, 1951), Chapter 8 "The Domain of Creativity, the Meaning of the Creative Act, the Creative Act as Ecstasy," p. 217

[4] Ibid , p. 213

[5] Aquinas, Thomas, *Summa Theologica* (Random House, 1948), edited by Anton C. Pegis, Creation, Question XLV "The Mode of Emanation of Things from the

First Principle," Fifth Article "Whether it Belongs to God Alone to Create?", p 243. Aquinas grounds his argument on the distinction between the creation of being and the instrumental action of one being upon another This is not some obscure point in Aquinas but is basic to his discussion of God's role in creation and to distinctions he makes between that role and the role played by creatures themselves. And it is a feature of his thinking that continues to pop up in the literature on evolution. See, for example, William E. Carroll's essay "Aquinas and the Big Bang," *First Things*, No. 97, November 1999, p. 19, right hand column.

[6] Numbers, Ronald L , *Darwinism Comes to America* (Harvard University Press, 1998), Chapter 1 "Darwinism and the Dogma of Separate Creations the Response of American Naturalists to Evolution," Section "Evolution and Religion," p. 41

[7] *The Princeton Theology 1812 - 1921*, Mark A. Noll, editor and compiler (Baker Book House, Grand Rapids, Michigan, 1983), excerpts from *What Is Darwinism?*, p. 148

[8] *Ibid* , pp 149 - 150

[9] Dawkins, Richard, *The Blind Watchmaker* (W W Norton & Company, New York, London, 1996), Chapter 9 "Puncturing punctuationism," p. 249

[10] Ibid., Chapter 1 "Explaining the very improbable," p. 1; Chapter 2 "Good design," pp. 21, 36

[11] Ibid., Chapter 1, p. 5

[12] Ibid , p 6

[13] The use of brain and mind interchangeably here is not accidental. The two seem sufficiently closely related that, in an absence of certain knowledge about which does what, it seems safe to employ them as synonyms. My own guess is that the brain has more to do with how sensory input is organized and structured while the mind more to do with basic awareness and rational thought, but that is no more than a guess

[14] Overman, Richard H., *Evolution and the Christian Doctrine of Creation* (the Westminster Press, Philadelphia, 1967), Chapter 1 "The Coming of Evolutionary Theory," section 3 "Temporalizing the Chain of Being," p. 24

[15] Ibid., section 2 "The Fullness of God's Creation," p. 21. In his footnote to this point Overman says that in the final edition of *Systema Naturae* (1776), Linnaeus suggested that new species might be formed by hybridization, or even by chance See, too, Colin Patterson's *Evolution* (Cornell University Press, Ithaca, New York, 1999), Chapter 13 "The hierarchy of life," section 1 "Classification," p 101

[16] Zimmer, Carl, *At the Water's Edge* (Simon & Schuster, 1998), Chapter 1 "After a Lost Balloon," pp. 10 - 13

[17] Numbers, Ronald L , *Darwinism Comes to America*, Chapter 1, Section "Why Evolution?", pp 45 - 46

[18] Ibid , p. 47 - 48

[19] Ibid., p. 48

[20] I should note that Ronald G. Larson, discussing the impact of mass die-offs have on the fitness level of a population, appeals to the same phrase when he concludes that in such cases luck rather than superior genes determines which organisms will survive and that hence mass die-offs can actually lower the fitness level of a population ("Viral Evolution: Climbing Mount Molehill?", section "Viral Evolution: A Modest Proposal for the "Blind Watchmaker:, p. 173, *Perspectives on Science and Christian Faith*, September 2000, Vol 52, No 3) Dr. Larson's point was not quite what I had in mind when I appealed to the passage as I wrote this chapter in early 1999, but I find his insights most arresting.

[21] Dennett, Daniel, *Darwin's Dangerous Idea* (Simon & Schuster, 1995), Chapter 4 "The Tree of Life," section 2 "Color-coding a Species on the Tree," p 95

[22] Patterson, *Evolution*, Chapter 14 "Proof and disproof; science and politics," section 4 "A metaphysical research programme?", p. 120.

[23] Interestingly enough, Darwin seems aware of this philosophical problem but applies it to creationists rather than to his own position. When discussing rudimentary organs he notes that those who believe in creation claim that rudimentary organs exist for the sake of symmetry. Darwin dismisses the claim as being "no explanation, merely a restatement of the fact" (Darwin, Charles, *The Origin of Species* [first edition published in 1859 and reprinted by Bantam in June, 1999], Chapter 13, "Mutual Affinities of Organic Beings: Morphology Embryology: Rudimentary Organs", p.370). Just so for the argument about survival of the fittest. It simply restates in a different form what is assumed But restatements in a different form are not explanations.

[24] We should note that metaphysical concepts alone do not exhaust the terminological difficulties that plague evolution theory. For example in *A Natural History of Rape* Randy Thornhill and Craig T. Palmer inform us that in order to demonstrate as plausible the claim that a trait was designed by natural selection, one must show that the trait performs its assumed function with sufficient precision, efficiency, and economy (Chapter 1, section "By-Products of Selection," p 10). However, plausibility is not proof and can always be doubted. Furthermore one wonders how sufficiency is quantified The authors never tell us.

[25] Patterson, *Evolution*, Chapter 14, p. 119. Popper argued that there is no law of evolution for human beings or for life in general Thus there is no law of evolution for science to disclose Instead there is simply the fact that change appears to have occurred. The idea that this change expresses some necessary character or points in a particular direction he attributes to a nineteenth century mistake whereby "Natural Law" was substituted for divine providence (*Conjectures and Refutations*, Part II Refutations, Chapter 16 "Prediction and Prophecy in the Social Sciences," Section v, p. 340). For a more in depth discussion of this substitution of natural law for divine providence, see my own *The Depersonalization of God* (University Press of America, 1989).

[26] Dawkins, *The Blind Watchmaker*, Chapter 10 "The one true tree of life," p. 271

[27] Ibid., Preface, p. xv, Chapter 2 "Good design," pp. 38, 41, Chapter 3 "Accumulating small change," pp. 43, 49, 56, Chapter 11 Doomed rivals," p 317

[28] Ibid., Chapter 6 "Origins and Miracles," p 146

[29] Ibid., Chapter 11, p. 304

[30] Ibid., p. 306

[31] Ibid., 304

[32] Gleick, James, *Chaos* (Penguin Books, 1987), Chapter 7 "The Experimenter," p. 201

[33] It would surprise many evolutionists as well. A great number among them view teleology as a logical fallacy based on seeing intention where none exists. Two points can be raised here. First, teleology does not necessarily imply intention, only the influence of final cause. Intention requires consciousness, and final causes may or may not be conscious. Second, how can one demonstrate the non-existence of intention, especially when evaluating systems which seem to be

designed to fulfill certain functions? One may claim that intention is absent, but such a claim is no more convincing than the claim that intention is present

[34] Thornhill, and Palmer, *A Natural History of Rape*, Chapter 1, section "Natural Selection and Adaptations," p. 6; Chapter 3 "Why Do Men Rape?", section "Rape and Evolutionary Agents," p 56, Chapter 5, section "The Historical Neglect of Adaptation," p 106. Here we are told that these four causes actually underlie microevolution. It is worth noting that macroevolution requires microevolution but does not necessarily follow from it.

[35] Ibid , Glossary, p. 209

[36] Ibid., Chapter 1, section "By-Products of Selection," p, 10

[37] Ibid., Glossary, p. 209

[38] Note that the claim that life needed to appear only once is a effort to reduce the odds against the development of life on earth. Among the countless organic molecules combining and recombining in primal conditions, only one needed to strike upon the proper combination of elements once in order to set in motion that chain of events that would eventually result in you and me

[39] I posted this question on the MSNBC science bulletin board in late 1999 and received the rather unenlightening reply. as many as it takes I suppose the poster wanted to suggest that the question as posed is unanswerable, but in principle it ought not to be And reflecting on it makes us aware of the huge number of changes involved, not just the transformation of limbs into flippers, or a snout into a blowhole, or tail into flukes, but changes involving fat distribution, the nervous system, the structure of internal organs and so forth. In short, what is being hypothesized is a transformation of exceedingly improbable scope.

[40] Zimmer, *At the Water's Edge*, chronology, p. 239

[41] Ibid., Chapter 7 "Along the Tethyan Shores" and Chapter 8 "Walking to Swimming"

[42] Ibid , Chapter 9 "A Voyage Out," p. 202

[43] Ibid., p. 200, chart on page 203, p. 215

[44] Ibid., p. 199. Zimmer quotes Phillip Gingerich as suggesting that perhaps *Pakicetus* and the first true whale are separated by only two million years and that only five million years stand between *Pakicetus* and *Ambulocetus*

[45] Dawkins, *The Blind Watchmaker*, Chapter 4 "Making tracks through animal space," p. 90

[46] Darwin, Charles, *The Origin of Species*, Chapter 1 "Variation Under Domestication," pp. 16 - 18; Chapter 8 "Hybridism," pp. 220 - 221; Patterson, *Evolution*, Chapter 3 "Variation within species," section 4 "Variation under domestication," p. 7. Strangely enough Darwin did not entertain such reservations about pigeons (*The Origin of Species*, Chapter 1, pp 21 - 24) though he argued that were some of the existing varieties shown to an ornithologist who was told they were wild, he would doubtless classify them as distinct species (p 21), and though he himself initially doubted that so many varieties of the bird could have come from one species (p 25) Nor did variety seem to bother Darwin when he argued in *The Descent of Man* (1871) that human beings and apes originated from a common ancestor some time between the Eocene and late Miocene epochs.

[47] In an attempt to determine how life might have originated, experiments have been conducted in which hypothesized early atmospheres were prepared and then subjected to ultraviolet radiation or electrical discharges Scientists have been conducting such experiments since 1953 when Stanley Miller, a doctoral student at the University of Chicago, did the first one by combining John Haldane's and Harold C. Urey's ideas about the early atmosphere. Subjecting an atmosphere of hydrogen, water, methane, and ammonia to an electric discharge, Miller devised a process that in a week was able to produce the amino acids glycine, glutamic acid, aspartic acid, and alanine. Since then cytosine and guanine have appeared among the many organic compounds scientists have synthesized as they have varied these "primal" atmospheres, but thymine has not formed. However uracil which is found in place of thymine in ribonucleic acid (RNA) has been generated in such experiments This is one reason some researchers believe that RNA may have originated prior to DNA, then developed in such a way as to create DNA based life. If this was the case as the failure of experimenters to design an experiment that would generate thymine suggests, then the origin of DNA based life faces an additional hurdle since the RNA template in addition to needing molecules of sugars with which to create a nucleotides would also need thymine Even given an environment in which such sugars abounded and thymine appeared, scientists have not found it easy to devise experiments that might have plausibly produced nucleotides. And even with the formation of nucleic acids, complex co-operative systems of proteins must still develop before we would have life as we know it. Proteins are built from amino acids. DNA can synthesize twenty such amino acids. A protein molecule is typically between 150 and 200 amino acids long. Each functioning somatic cell in a human body contains at a minimum 10,000 different kinds of protein How likely is it that something so inconceivably complex could have developed from the mindless interplay of natural forces?

[48] This is a thesis Popper develops in *The Logic of Scientific Discovery* and to which he refers in *Conjectures and Refutations*, Part I, Chapter 1, Section x, pp 57 - 58; Chapter 3 "Three Views Concerning Human Knowledge," Section 3 "The First View: Ultimate Explanation by Essence," pp. 103 - 105, Section 5 "Criticism of the Instrumentalist View,' p. 112; Section 6 "The Third View: Conjectures, Truth, and Reality," pp. 114 - 115. In replying to G. S Kirk in his Appendix to Chapter 5 "Back to the Presocratics," Popper insists that he assumes there is such a thing as absolute scientific truth, but that though we may approach it we cannot be sure we have reached it (Section i, p. 157), a point he reiterates in Chapter 6 "A Note on Berkeley as Precursor to Mach and Einstein," Sec v, p 174, when in distinguishing his view from the views of essentialists and positivists he claims that scientists aim at constructing theories that are true descriptions of phenomena even though they cannot be sure they have succeeded.

[49] Popper, *Conjectures and Refutations*, Part I, Chapter 1, Section vii, p. 51. Indeed, he argues that it is a mistake to attribute even a high degree of probability to scientific theory. All we can really say is that a particular theory is an attempt to describe a particular thing and has stood up to such tests as we have contrived for it. But, he points out, it can be shown mathematically that corroboration cannot be equated with mathematical probability and that all theories, even the best, have a mathematical probability of zero (Chapter 8, Section 1, p. 192).

[50] Popper argued that none of the sources of our knowledge have authority (*Conjectures and Refutations*, Introduction, Section xiv, p. 24; Section xv, p. 25). For Popper the problem to be solved is not the problem of authority since all our knowledge is human knowledge, it is instead how can we admit that our knowledge is human and still rescue it from arbitrariness? To this end, appealing to Xenophanes, Democritus, and Socrates, he proposes that we must unstintingly subject our theses to tireless rational criticism (Section x, p. 16) He goes on to argue that a dogmatic or pseudo-scientific attitude toward truth betrays itself in a tendency to seek ways to verify theses, whereas a critical attitude, which he identifies as a scientific one, looks for possible ways to falsify theses (Chapter 1 "Science Conjectures and Refutations," Section vii, p. 50).

[51] Of course some wag might say, "Your name is Ben Carter. You come from Irving, Texas. You purpose to write this book. Your destiny is the grave And meaning is what is important to you." But no one (not even, one supposes, the wag) who has begun to ask such questions will find such facile answers, true as they might be in their limited scope, satisfying because the issues addressed by such questions extend far beyond what the answers provide The wag (turned serious) may respond that such issues are based on illusions and that our questions consequent to such illusions are wrongheaded. This may be true, but as such questions grow out of our existential situations and seem to be universal among our species, it is not clear that the issues are illusions or that the questions

are wrongheaded. Indeed, one might argue that they are evidence of our fundamentally metaphysical character, that, as the Preacher said, all we do is vanity, and yet God has placed eternity in our hearts (Ecclesiastes 1:2 - 3; 3:11).

[52] My thesis if accepted would not solve these problems, but then I am not claiming that my system is a foundational integrative principle for contemporary biology.

[53] For all its flaws, and there are many, *Fundamentalisms Observed* (edited by Martin Marty and R. Scott Appleby, University of Chicago Press, 1991) makes this point very clear. For example, Gideon Aran in his essay "Jewish Zionist Fundamentalism: the Bloc of Faithful in Israel" notes that fundamentalism is inextricably intertwined with modernity (p. 330), and Manning Nash in his essay ""Islamic Resurgence in Malaysia" draws the conclusion that the movement he studied is neither anti-technological or anti-scientific (p. 733).

[54] Many in the New Age Movement, for example, are critical of science even as they embrace various theories about evolution and interpret those theories in the most creative ways to illustrate their own visions of reality

[55] Moorehead, Alan, *Darwin and the Beagle* (Harper & Row, 1969), Chapter 1 "The Meeting," pp. 22, 25

[56] I mention the time frame because, though the precise figures are not necessarily important, vast age as a general assertion is so essential to the theory.

[57] Patterson, *Evolution*, Chapter 13 "The hierarchy of life," section 3 "Molecular evolution," p. 111

[58] Ibid., section 1 "Classification," p. 101

[59] Nor was he so far removed from the biblical account. The idea that kind will bring forth after its kind suggests that life was endowed with the property of replication without direct divine intervention at each generation

[60] Patterson, *Evolution*, Chapter 15 "The origin and early evolution of life," section 1 "Prokaryotes and eukaryotes," p. 124

[61] Dawkins, *The Blind Watchmaker*, Chapter 2 "Good design," p. 38; Chapter 4, p. 86. He calls this kind of argument "extremely weak" and "pathetic." It may well be however that the "Just So" stories are themselves weak and pathetic. After all, they serve their purpose if they appear plausible, and they achieve plausibility in part by appealing to assumptions and in part by appealing to ignorance In other words, "Just So" stories are radically system dependent In effect the tale spinner says: "We don't know, but here is a possibility." Of course

mere possibility is by definition inconclusive. The skeptic who claims not to be able to imagine a particular scenario is demanding not speculation but demonstration. Thus the skeptic rather than the enthusiast bears the torch of science for science feeds of skepticism and is always fascinated by the unknown

[62] Shipman, Pat, *Taking Wing* (Simon & Schuster, New York, 1998), Chapter 5 "A Bird in the Hand," p. 126

[63] Ibid., Chapter 6 "Birds of a Feather," p 153. I confess I have more trouble imagining how down might have been created in the way Prof. Shipman, an anthropologist, suggests, but I am not an anthropologist

[64] Ibid , 159

[65] Ibid., Chapter 7 "On the Wing," p. 167, Chapter 8 "One Fell Swoop," p. 185 And even fossils, as I suggest below, prove far less than we might like to believe.

[66] Umberto Eco wove his novel *The Name of the Rose* around this point   Think of it as a parable for our time.

[67] Such creationist revisionism has taken dozens of forms, but for a particularly sophisticated example see "Genesis Reconsidered" by Armin Held and Peter Rust in *Perspectives on Science and Christian Faith*, Volume 51, Number 4, December 1999.

[68] Popper's theory of science is again apropos   He argues that science as it is actually done is not based on observation but on conjectures which are tested by observations, and that to be scientific such observations should be selected with the goal of falsifying the conjecture (*Conjectures and Refutations*, Chapter 1, Section iv and v, p. 46). Of course with the fossil record one cannot select one's observations, one simply discovers what the strata hold. Thus the procedure is not one of seeking to falsify conjectures so much as it is one of seeking to describe what one has found in light of one's earlier conjectures. This, Popper would argue, creates two problems. First, predictions based on the perceived progression of forms in the rocks are so vague that they amount to little more than soothsaying (he applies this criticism to both astrology and Marxism [Section ii, p 37]). Second, the observations tend to be interpreted in light of earlier observations which they are then imagined to confirm (a criticism he applies to Marxism and psychoanalysis [Section 1, p. 35]). It is easy, he observes, to obtain confirmations for theories if we look for confirmations. Only confirmations of results we should not have expected had we not known of the theory should be accorded any significance (p. 36).

[69] Zimmer, *At the Water's Edge*, Chapter 2 "Limitless Air, Ho!", pp. 35 - 37

[70] Biologists have even descended into those depths to watch coelacanths swim by "walking" through the water

[71] Zimmer, *At the Water's Edge*, Chapter 2, p. 46

[72] Lavoisier (1743 - 1794) was the first to introduce quantitative methods into the study of chemistry. For this innovation he is remembered as one of the founders of modern chemistry. He was guillotined during the French Revolution.

[73] Zimmer, *At the Water's Edge*, Chapter 6 "The Equation of a Whale," p 158

Chapter 3

Strange Science

<u>Introduction</u>

It was a great moment in the history of science. Sir Arthur Stanley Eddington, cosmologist, astronomer, and physicist, had organized an experiment to test Einstein's prediction that light would bend if it passed by a massive body. In anticipation of a solar eclipse in 1919 Sir Eddington sent observers to Principe, an island in the Gulf of Guinea off the west African coast, and to Sobral in Brazil with instructs to direct their telescopes toward the edge of the sun. If Einstein was right, the eclipse, by blotting out most of the sun's light, would reveal at the sun's edge stars known to be behind the sun. This would happen as light from those stars curved around the sun, making them visible to the observers on earth. And sure enough when eclipse occurred the stars could be seen just as Einstein had predicted.[1] Popper, describing his thrill at the results, relates that the experiment had a lasting effect on his intellectual development.[2] The experiment has been duplicated many times and no one doubts the reality of the phenomenon, but what is not generally appreciated is that the results of the 1919 experiment were far more ambiguous than tradition indicates. An overcast sky at Principe meant that only two of the plates made could be used. In Sobral a poorly focused telescope produced eight useable plates, and another produced eighteen that were not as good. The deflections calculated by astronomers from those eighteen plates were in line with the predictions of classical physics while the calculations based on the eight better plates from the poorly focused telescope were much higher than Einstein predicted. However, by factoring in the results of the two plates from Principe and using a method that assumed some of what he expected to find, Eddington was able to derive a deflection value close to the one predicted by Einstein. That was the value Eddington presented as a triumph.[3] Sometimes one can be so confident that one can feel justified in fudging the figures. After all, experiments like the one described above are expensive, hard to organize, and contingent upon conditions that occur infrequently, so why not opt for the dramatic announcement?

A Record of Dishonesty and Intolerance

In Chapter One we argued that current developments in neurobiology have given new credibility to the philosophical traditions of structuralism or conceptualism, thus revitalizing a Kantian epistemological critique of knowledge. We then discussed how this impacts and humbles the model building tendency of contemporary science. In Chapter Two we described how the current cultural milieu coupled with this model building tendency encourages the application of evolution theory to draw conclusions unsupported by hard science, and we argued that the scenarios consequent to such applications are evidence of nothing. In this chapter we will show how in defending such expansions scientists have in public claimed a certainty for the theory of evolution which they knew it failed to attain, and in the process have evidenced conspicuous intolerance. All this has been done at the very time advocates for evolution were accusing their opponents of the same sins: misrepresentation and intolerance. To illuminate the mindset behind such dishonesty, we will begin by relating three revealing episodes The first revolves around a claim made by a group of reputable scientists in 1985 that *Archaeopteryx*, the famous fossil of the earliest bird, was a hoax. In retelling this story I do not wish to imply that I think the fossils are hoaxes. I do not believe they are. But what I find interesting is the vitriol released by merely raising the possibility. After all, there was nothing new about the charge, and the research it inspired generated useful data.[4]

We should begin by noting that only seven specimens of *Archaeopteryx* are known,[5] all come from the Bavarian region of Germany,[6] and two, the Solnhofen and the Solnhofer Aktien-Verein specimens, were discovered after the academic rumpus erupted.[7]

Now to the story: in 1985 Sir Fred Hoyle and N. Chandra Wickramasinghe, two astrophysicists at University College in Cardiff, Wales, and both well known critics as Darwinism, a physicist, R. S. Watkins, also of University College in Cardiff, and two other physicists John Watkins and Lee Spetner of Israel who was also an expert in electronics, published four articles in the *British Journal of Photography* (March 8, March 29, April 26, and June 21) arguing that *Archaeopteryx* was a hoax.[8] The charges had been leveled before. The fossil was found in 1861, just two years after Darwin published *On the Origin of Species* and one year after it had come out in German. Whereas evolution met with a fairly friendly audience in Britain, there was much opposition to the idea in Germany, and this opposition doubtless increased skepticism about the fossil. In 1862 the original owner of the fossil, a physician and amateur fossil collector named Carl Haberlein, sought to raise money for his daughter's dowry by auctioning his collection of which *Archaeopteryx* was the most important piece. In order to heighten interest, he shrouded *Archaeopteryx* in mystery, allowing no one to photographic it or even to sketch it. This secrecy along with the fact that the collection was being sold and contained this incredible half-bird, half-reptile specimen that seemed so conveniently to bolster Darwin's theory engendered speculation that the piece was a clever forgery.[9] In 1877 when a second *Archaeopteryx* fossil was discovered and within weeks acquired by Ernst Haberlein, Dr. Carl Haberlein's son, who, like his father, decided to sell it. Again there was speculation that the specimen was a forgery.[10] What the researchers in 1985 claimed to have found was evidence that these old charges were true.

The researchers based their conclusion on three observations. First, they noted that while the bones were embedded in limestone, the feather impressions seemed to have been made in a thin layer with a significantly different composition than the rest of the rock. Second, they noted that some of the imprints seem to have been made by feathers which were first pressed down, then lifted, moved over slightly and pressed down again. This had been observed by Sir Gavin de Beer as early as 1954 though he was unable to explain the phenomenon. To the researchers it looked suspiciously like a forger's error. Third, they noted that when the two halves of the stone containing the fossil were placed together, the fossils were not perfect images of one another.[11]

Paleontologists immediately went on the attack. Their rebuttal was based on four arguments. First, they pointed out that since limestone is laid down slowly in layers the thin layer with the feather impressions was exactly what one would expect.[12] Second, they brought forward other specimens of *Archaeopteryx* that were found under unsuspicious circumstances and also show the feather markings.[13] Third, they noted that the differences between the halves of the specimen the researchers examined were slight and could be accounted for if one assumed the fossil had been damaged when the rock containing it was split.[14] Finally, they argued that what the researchers saw as "double-stuck" feathers could be explained if one assumed that *Archaeopteryx* had a double row of primary feathers.[15]

What is striking about this debate, however, was its acrimony and the uncooperative stance assumed by the British Museum once the researchers published. After all, the men, though not working in their fields, were highly respected scientists who conducted their investigation in a thoroughly scientific way. Recall, too, that the research that was done produced valuable data and ultimately verified the authenticity of the fossils. Yet, once the curators found out what the researchers were up to, they refused to provide samples, or provided samples that were too small for the researchers to work with, or refused to conduct their own tests on the fossils. The Catholic Church was more opened to investigators who wanted to examine the Turin Shroud than the British Museum was to those who wanted to look at its own icons. Their fury is reminiscent of Karl Popper's remark, referred to in the last chapter, that the desire to be right is a sign of those who have the wrong view of science. People so exercised appear less like seekers of truth and more like passionate believers in a particular faith.

And they treat dissent much as believers might, as our next two examples will show. Michael Behe tells the story of Forrest Mims, a science writer who in 1990 was invited to write several guest columns for "Amateur Scientist," a regular feature in *Scientific American*. It was understood that if the columns were well received, Mims would be offered a position at the magazine. No problems were expected as Mims was well qualified, and none were encountered until Mims was invited for his final interview. During that interview he was asked if he believed in evolution, an odd question surely. Since when do scientists "believe in" theories? Mims responded that he did not, that he believed in the biblical account of creation. As a consequence he was not hired. The magazine was concerned that supplementing its writing pool with creationist talent would compromise its status as a scientific journal.[16]

Of course one might try to justify the magazine's decision by arguing that Forrest Mims was only a science writer, not a true research scientist, and that the administrators responsible for staffing were not trying to suppress ideas but simply keep the publication free of religious proselytism that would be inappropriate in a neutral setting like the one provided by *Scientific American*.[17] Religion, so the argument might run, is one thing, science quite another. Setting aside for the moment the civil rights issues involved in such an argument (are secular employers to be allowed to take religious affiliation into account when making hiring decisions?), notice how it collapses in the case of Dean H. Kenyon who is not only a research scientist but one of the leaders in his field.

Dr. Kenyon earned his Ph.D. in biophysics from Stanford University and became a Professor of Biology at San Francisco State University as well as the Coordinator of its General Biology Program. In 1969 he co-authored *Biochemical Predestination*, a standard work on how life may have originated in an undirected way in an environment that might have existed billions of years ago. During the 1970s most of his published research, some of it conducted at NASA-Ames Research Center, dealt with this question. But by the late 1970s, confronting a growing body of experimental evidence that suggested complex information-bearing molecules do not arise spontaneously from simpler components, he began to doubt that they could. It seemed to him that instead of investigating the problem of how life might have arisen in some spontaneous way, the researchers were planing experiments that produced the results they desired, that the experiments were not modeling a plausible natural process as they purported to do, but instead were fashioned to bring about a predetermined outcome. Thus the experiments revealed nothing about the spontaneous organization of matter and everything about imposed design. By the 1980s Kenyon had come to the view that life showed evidence of having been designed, and he began to discuss the experiment's negative results with his students, describe his concerns, and point to weaknesses in the theory of evolution.[18] Eventually some of the students complained and John Hafernik, the chairman of the biology department, stepped in, ordering Kenyon to stop teaching "biblical creationism" in class. In the exchange that followed, Kenyon requested clarification, was told to teach the dominate view, insisted that he did but that he also pointed out problems with it, then was taken out of class and banished to the laboratory. The San Francisco State University's Academic Freedom Committee and the American Association of University Professors both came to Dean Kenyon's defense, but John Hafernik was unmoved, insisting that he was within his rights and exercising his responsibility to determine what constituted appropriate scientific content in the university's classrooms.[19]

Notice that the scientific competence of Forrest Mims and Dean Kenyon was never questioned, nor was their approach to science challenged. Instead they came to grief because they drew conclusions that not only ran counter to the dominate view but were deemed at the outset to be beyond bounds, conclusions which in Forrest Mims' case would have had no direct impact on the work he was expected to do. Nor was the truth or falsity of those conclusions at issue. It was instead the idea that God or some other outside agent might have had a hand in creation that was deemed not only inappropriate for scientific inquiry but as justifying the silencing of those who entertain such notions. Design as a possibility could not even be considered without jeopardizing one's career. The herd of independent minds dislikes having its philosophical presuppositions questioned as much as it dislikes having its icons examined.

Indeed, so great is this dislike, so great is the desire among evolutionists to prevail in the current cultural debate, that they not above mendacity. To illustrate: when Darwin wrote, nothing was known of genetics. While he never publicly agreed with Lamarck, Darwin was influenced by Lamarck's ideas if only because those ideas had no real rival for presenting a plausible vehicle for explaining population change,[20] and as time passed, Darwin became increasingly Lamarckian,[21] so much so that he can by some standards be called a neo-Lamarckian.[22] Indeed, early in the debate, many of Darwin's champions defended evolution not by appealing to natural selection but by appealing to Lamarck. The American philosopher Chauncey Wright noted the phenomenon and remarked at the time that Darwin had won a victory not for himself but for Lamarck.[23] When Gregor Mendel first published in 1864, the significance of his work was unappreciated. It was not until 1900 that William Bateson, who coined the word *genetics*, along with Hugo de Vries and others first realized the importance of what Mendel measured while he cross-fertilized his garden peas. However, as the new science of genetics progressed, investigators began to appreciate that natural selection, rather than encouraging the development of new characteristics, tended instead to stabilize populations by eliminated mutations from the gene pool. This was because most mutations had a negative influence and interfered with the reproductive success of the organisms that carried them or, if they had a positive influence, it was insufficient to provide an advantage significant enough for them to establish themselves. Thus natural selection worked to retard change in large successfully reproducing populations. This was not what Darwin had predicted. Hence during the first quarter of the twentieth century, natural selection was not highly regarded as a credible means by which evolution might occur.[24] And, since the 1880s when the zoologist August Weismann tested it and found he could not verify it, Lamarckism had been out of favor as well.[25] For these reasons that, William Bateson, when speaking to a convention of the American Association for the Advancement of Science in 1921, admitted agnosticism about how new species came into existence, but insisted nevertheless that the fossil record undergirded his faith that evolution had occurred.[26]

Bateson's word *faith* is an honest one, but rings strangely in the bell jar of science. After all, faith was associated with the tissue of religion, but here it was the tissue that unified scattered fossils into a record, then interpreted that record, and lifted the result over the mathematical objections of the geneticists. The fossils seen as a progression suggested that something was happening. If it wasn't natural selection, it could be called evolution anyway since evolution, at a minimum, meant change.

During these decades the fundamentalists had organized and were on the march, and debunking evolution was one of their ambitions. Many in the scientific community saw fundamentalism as anti-intellectual and a threat to science. It followed then that evolution must be defended, not because it was especially credible but because defending the theory was deemed necessary to protect science and civilized culture in general. Thus eminent scientists and intellectuals were quick to array themselves in defense of Darwin, not because they found Darwin especially credible at the time but because they believed by defending his thesis that they were defending science itself.[27] While the good citizens of Dayton, Tennessee, were outspoken in their confidence that the Bible is true, the defenders of the future tucked their faith behind the veil of empiricism and reason. They saw this as a clash between progress and superstition, and they were confident that their descendants would understand the purpose of their hyperbole. History, they believed, was on their side and would justify them. And anyway they held the reigns of power.

But the fact is that at Dayton, Tennessee, the courthouse rang not as superstition clashed with science but as faith struggled with faith – and the scientists knew it.[28] They knew that the tide of knowledge at the time seemed to have turned against evolution if only because they could find no plausible mechanism to explain how the process might occur, but they hid that fact from the general public because it was important to win. This was not the last time that evolutionists worried that veracity would jeopardize their case.

The late Colin Patterson, who worked in the Paleontology Department at the British Museum of Natural History from 1962 until his retirement in 1993[29] and whose text on evolution is a standard in the field and one to which we have already referred, learned the hard way of the dangers of honesty when, in 1981, while lecturing at the American Museum of Natural History, he questioned the confidence evolutionists placed on the data that undergirded their theory, and noted how unsure they were (at this late date!) of the mechanisms behind the process. He went on to characterize both creation and evolution as empty and pseudo-scientific concepts.[30] If he sought to be provocative, he succeeded. While creationists seized upon the lecture, evolutionists responded with a storm of protest. Of the incident Patterson, who notes the skepticism that his own predecessor Errol White expressed toward evolution in an address delivered in the 1960s to the Linnaean Society of London of which he was then president,[31] writes that he learned how dangerous "candour in argument" was since by being truthful one might bolster the case of the creationists.[32]

Indeed, academics sympathetic to evolution have in its defense occasionally falsified the history of the conflict. Mary Midgley, formerly Senior Lecturer in Philosophy at the University of Newcastle upon Tyne and long time nemesis of Richard Dawkins,[33] notes that our version of the 1860 debate between Thomas H. Huxley and Bishop Wilberforce is at variance with the accounts written at the time. The famous remark made by Bishop Wilberforce about Prof. Huxley's ancestors, and Prof. Huxley's reply, attracted so little attention that they were not recorded. Instead they were recalled later. Indeed, she observers that the chronicle of the debate reveals that Bishop Wilberforce participated not as a clergyman but as a credible ornithologist, a representative of the great anatomist Sir Richard Owen, and vice-president of the British Academy. His objections to Darwin's theory were not emotional but scientific, and the man who actually answered those objections was not Huxley but the botanist Joseph Hooker. Midgley is generous enough to suggest that Huxley's account of the affair was not intentionally dishonest but was the result of a faulty memory.[34] That may be, but it is difficult to countenance the survival for over a century of Huxley's faulty version.

Dawkins himself is not above a little historical fabrication. In *The Blind Watchmaker* he refers twice to "fake human footprints" which he says were carved in the dinosaur beds of Texas during the Depression to trick tourists.[35] In fact, in 1986, the same year that *The Blind Watchmaker* came out, Glen J. Kuban, a computer programmer and expert in dinosaur footprints, announced, after a five year investigation of the Paluxy River tracks, that they were not hoaxes. Instead the tracks were dinosaur prints that had been smoothed and distorted by natural irregularities, erosion, or as sediment settled into them. Kuban also suggested that the dinosaurs who made the prints walked, not on their toes as dinosaurs were generally believed to do, but by placing the full weight on their soles into the ground. After examining the evidence, many paleontologists agreed, and creationists withdrew their film about the tracks entitled *Footprints in Stone*.[36] However, in subsequent editions of *The Blind Watchmaker* (1987, 1996), Dawkins does not correct his statement. In his book the footprints remain fakes carved during the Depression to trick tourists (such specificity makes fiction sound so true) and the creationists remain excited about them. After all, one cannot let facts, regardless of how interesting they are, stand in the way of a story, no matter how silly it is (are we really to believe that no one would notice the tracks were carved?), especially when the story allows one to take a poke at creationists.

But anti-creationists have not only falsified the history of the debate, they have been willing to fudge some of the classic data used to illustrate evolution theory as well. Two examples should suffice to make the point. First, most of us who took biology in high school in mid-twentieth century America were taught the doctrine of common descent and will recall the illustration of vertebrate embryos arranged side by side that was used as evidence for the doctrine. What we did not know at the time was that the artist had amplified supposed similarities among the embryos. As the artist's embellishments have become more generally recognized, most biology texts since the 1980s have withdrawn that famous picture, but the fact remains that it was used for several decades in standard American high school texts despite that fact that many biologists were well aware of the picture's misleading character.

Second, peppered moths (*Biston betularia*) have long been used to illustrate a type of variation within species known as "industrial melanism."[37] The argument, first proposed in 1896 by J.W. Tutt, runs thus: peppered moths rest on tree trunks. The whitish lichens that cover the tree trunks in unpolluted areas provide camouflage for lighter peppered moths who blend into the background afforded by the lichens while the occasional darker peppered moths are more easily visible against the lichens and more often eaten by birds. Hence in unpolluted areas lighter colored moths are dominate. However, as industrial pollution kills the lichens, the denuded and darker tree trunks provide better camouflage for the darker moths and the advantages of the lighter and darker varieties are reversed. Hence in polluted areas darker moths predominate. And we remember, again from our high school texts, photographs of dark and light peppered moths against lichens and against bare trunks. It is now known, however, that peppered moths do not normally rest on tree trunks. Instead they beneath smaller branches high in the woodland canopy. In fact, the photos used as evidence of natural selection were staged. Dead moths were glued to the trunks of trees where they do not normally rest. While industrial melanism does in fact seem to be a genuine phenomenon and while predation may be a factor in its occurrence, we can now be fair certain that the explanation suggested over a hundred years ago by Tutt is wrong, yet that explanation, though it initially seemed to be confirmed by experiments conducted in the 1950s by Bernard Kettewell, has since the 1980s been thoroughly discredited.[38] Notice this: even had Tutt been right, his argument would have proved nothing about the origin of species since what he was attempting to account for was not the emergence of a new species but variety within a species. Notice, too, that his proposal stood for almost a century before enough was known about how peppered moths actually behave to evaluate the hypothesis, and when enough was known the hypothesis was found wanting. This is not to disparage Tutt. What he proposed was reasonable, given what was known at the time. And his proposal provided a framework for productive experiments that eventually increased our knowledge about peppered moths. That is science. The problem is that the cryptic coloration and selective predation model which Tutt proposed is now known to be inadequate. The photos illustrating it are known to have been staged. And yet it continues to be used as an evidence of evolution, even though had it been correct all it would have been evidence of is variation within species.

The Problem

What kind of science is it that treats its challengers so? On one hand, it could be argued that this is nothing new, that from its inception science has produced leading lights who, when they had power, abused that power. Sir Isaac Newton is a notorious example. One of the greatest scientists who ever lived and the first to be knighted, he was nevertheless an unpleasant person who often engaged in acrimony and was not above using his authority as president of the Royal Society to coerce other members or to suppress work with which he disagreed. On the other hand, the examples we have looked at go far beyond the life of a single person or the compass of a single generation. They seem instead to point to something endemic in the enterprise itself. The science of evolution is in this sense a bit like archeology, filled with petty rivalries, small jealousies, and venomous exchanges. It is in short one of the historical disciplines and as such goes beyond the experimentation and immediate observation that mediates disputes in the more traditional sciences.[39] After all, if one disagrees with a colleague over the behavior of an element under certain conditions, one can create those conditions and observe the element. But with sciences like evolution and archeology things are not so simple. Here the evidence is far more indirect, far more ambiguous, and far more tied to the egos of those investigating problems. After all, when people have spent their lives exploring and defending a particular position, being right can become more important than disclosing truth. Ideally science should progress via falsification. A thesis is proposed and then either those who propose it strive along with their colleagues to prove it wrong. Those these which survive the assault are assumed to be provisionally true. They become theories to be abandoned when better theories are devised. But in the case of evolution, scientists have rallied not to disprove the theory but to prove it. Corroborative evidence not contradictory evidence is sought. Problems with the theory are explained away, a not too difficult enterprise since evolution is a very complex story and problems with complex stories can always be ironed out by adding or subtracting complexities.

A historical discipline, evolution is heir to three key dilemmas. First, as we argued in the last chapter, it is greatly dependent on interpretation which means it is more easily influenced by cultural paradigms than are other sciences.

Second, it is forever fixed to the peculiar inadequacy of its own data. Relying as heavily as they do on the fossil record, evolution scenarios remain highly tentative since a single discovery can overturn an entire system of ideas. Consider the problem it would pose were the imprint of a feather found in Carboniferous shales. Of course an evolutionist might insist this will never occur, and the evolutionist may well be right, but there is no way to prove one will not come to light tomorrow – or in a thousand years.[40]

Finally, the possibilities embraced by such scenarios are bounded by the possibilities limned in our own minds. For example, Dawkins, like many evolutionists, believes that the world we perceive is a virtual reality the brain weaves from incomplete sensory data,[41] a simulated world that is kept in perfect synchrony with the real world,[42] a picture world that is species specific.[43] He even suggests, echoing Gunther Stent with whom we began in chapter one, that certain aspects of reality may be forever closed to us because our brains are not constituted so as to understand them.[44] I am happy to confess that I agree with him here, yet I find it strange that he seems to miss how such a conceit undermines his efforts to accurately model the past. Such an epistemology not only means that we interact with a "human world" rather than the world as it is, it also means that a knowledge of initial conditions is forever closed to us as is a knowledge of how events develop from those conditions. Of course we may catch glimpses of things, but those glimpses are humanized, constructed by our brains from incomplete sensory data. The really significant things may be as invisible to us as art is invisible to a cat.

It is only through the present that we have access to the past. We guess at its contours as we ponder the fragments it has left us, but we sense that the past was an alien place, another country, a different world. Understanding the alien past is not easy, so it is very tempting to project the familiar present onto it in an effort to make sense of things (the principle of uniformitarianism). We drape its fragments in a hologram of our imagination, and they live! Change the composition of the fragments, and the actors leap to conform to their new roles. Thus historical disciplines share much with the arts, and this sets them apart from more traditional sciences. An elegant experiment in electronics may have much of the craftsman about it, but it is qualitatively different from painting a picture, yet painting a picture is precisely what the historical sciences strive to do. But the picture painted is the one that exists in the mind of the historical scientist. It does not necessarily express the mind of God (though it may give one a sense of having a demigod's eye view of things) nor does it necessarily mirror the past. It is a more-or-less plausible imaginary construct. It can be nothing more. Of course contemplating that picture world may be aesthetically pleasing. That is a trait it shares with any art. And doubtless those who enjoy such pleasures are loathe to surrender them. And certainly they do not wish to exchange their pictures for the icons of other religions.

"Consilience of induction"

In his review of Johnson's *Darwin on Trial*, Gould observes that historical sciences are not generally experimental. Instead other methodologies are employed. The approach Darwin adopted, for example, was "consilience of induction" whereby a single consistent explanation was sought that would explain a broad and dissimilar assortment of data.[45] Such an explanation need not initially be particularly credible. Its credibility comes instead from its perceived capacity to explain the events in question. The more it is believed to explain, the more credibility the interpretive structure enjoys. In this way it becomes the explanatory paradigm by default.

Notice that Darwin appeals to inductive logic. It is important to remember that, as opposed to deductive logic where conclusions follow necessarily from the premises, in inductive logic conclusions, though supported by the premises, do not follow from them necessarily. When Darwin appealed to inductive logic, he was invoking a sound scientific principle. Science relies primarily on inductive logic which is why experiment and immediate observation are so consequential within the discipline. It is also important to remember that an explanation to be scientific should not appeal to agencies outside the scope of the material realm. It follows then that a scientific theory of origins will assume the sufficient efficacy of secondary and material causality, but the inductive nature of the discipline means that appeals to inevitability (Dawkins) or teleology (Gleick) are misplaced. In historical sciences events develop from initial conditions not necessarily but continently. It also follows that other viable possibilities are intentionally ignored. The goal of historical sciences is not to describe what actually occurred but to structure events within a proposed model so as to validate the model. Thus the intent is to verify not falsify the paradigm. Of course one can verify or falsify scenarios derived from the paradigm, but the larger thesis, that one can construct an adequate account of events by appealing exclusively to material and secondary causality, is sacrosanct.

Alfred North Whitehead once observed that science is more changeable than theology.[46] The comparison is interesting, the conclusion probably wrong. Theologies, like scientific scenarios, are malleable things. They come and go. Even the core truths around which theologies are spun have proved more pliant than the rock-ribbed conclusions of experimental science. We know how to engineer a bridge or a jet. Religion for its part enshrines mystery. Nevertheless evolution shares much with theology: it addresses the question of origin, it situates humanity in the universe,[47] it offers tools to those who wish to falsify biblical accounts, it undermines traditional theological arguments based on design, and, as Dawkins claims, it makes atheism intellectually fulfilling.[48] Evolution theory changes, and its transformations reflect its place in history and culture. We learn more, and we develop different interpretive tools to evaluate what we know. The facts change and accumulate, and as they do, the picture we construct alters dramatically.

However, the world we see is not necessarily the world that is. I do not mean by this that "reality is an illusion." Reality by definition cannot be an illusion. But our perception of the real, especially if we absolutize it, can lead us into illusion. What we see, and what we think about what we see, do not necessarily reflect what is. We humanize our world in order to comprehend it and our comprehension of it remains a human comprehension. Of course our brains model our immediate environment sufficiently well to enable us to survive in it. The brains of any successful species that have a brain must do as much. But when we attempt to reach into environments more removed from our immediate one, we begin to misperceive, introduce variables, get the picture wrong. And I suspect that the more removed from the immediate we are, the more distorted our view becomes.

The theories we construct, based upon our perceptions and thoughts, express higher level generalizations in which illusion and reality are often indistinguishably intermingled. If the theories reveal their practical value via experimentation and application, then their imaginary aspects are of secondary importance. For purely practical concerns *why* matters less than *how*. But if the theories serve a primarily descriptive/interpretative function, then their imaginary elements become definitive, especially as those theories serve as the foundation for subsequent broader generalizations. We project our own perspective into reality and structure that reality around it. We attempt to make the messy fuzziness of the world more comprehensible by reducing, simplifying, and eliminating it. And, as the examples at the beginning of this chapter illustrate, perhaps we are tempted not to look too closely at the evidence. We may even on occasion be enticed to corrupt the data in small ways to strengthen our own case. But that means that in the end the theories we construct are only stories we tell ourselves to make
sense (a human sense) of a universe we have humanized. As stories they may be interesting, even entertaining, but we err if we take them very seriously.

Thus evolution becomes another creation myth not so different in kind from earlier myths including, if you will, the Hebrew one. This does not mean that evolution theory is not a valuable research tool. We noted in the last chapter that Popper referred to it as a metaphysical research program. But we should notice how evolution and the historical sciences generally, particularly because the assume a story form, differ in kind from the physical sciences. Popper argues that science begins with myth.[49] Myths of course are quintessentially stories. Theology also begins with stories. Popper contends that science differs from myth in that science is willing to critically evaluate the myths or stories with which it works and to discard elements in those myths or stories which fail to stand up to rigorous analysis and to replace them with elements that stand up better. Science so conceived is akin to theology since theology, too, is willing to critically evaluate its stories. Indeed, it is part of my thesis that in the historical sciences, the sciences that are expressed as stories, the kinship between science and theology is especially prominent. This is because, though in the historical sciences the various stories might change, the underlying mechanism remains inviolable: the hand of God has been replace by secondary causality, the world of spirit is denied a role in the world of matter.

In the first part of this book I have attempted to build the case that evolution theory as it stands today is myth rather than science. In the second part of this book I will attempt to show how that myth, if treated as science, can be falsified as science. To this end I will discuss communication phenomena, arguing that we cannot account for it by appealing exclusively to processes of natural selection, that instead the ability to communicate is not only evidence of a soul, it is also evidence of God best understood in terms of Trinity.

Endnotes

[1] Silver, Brian L., *The Ascent of Science* (Oxford University Press, 1998), Part VIII, Chapter 32 "Relativity," Section "General Relativity," p 431

[2] Popper, Karl, *Conjectures and Refutations*, Part I, Chapter 1, Section I, p 34

[3] Morton, Oliver, "Science in the Dark," *The Wall Street Journal*, Vol CIV, No 29, Wednesday, August 11, 1999, p. A18

[4] Shipman, *Taking Wing*, Chapter 6, p. 148

[5] Ibid, Prologue "A Flight of Fancy," p. 13   Other early fossil "birds" were uncovered shortly thereafter. In 1870, for example, the American paleontologist

O C. Marsh while exploring Cretaceous strata in Kansas uncovered what he took to be the remains of a toothed bird. Christened *Hesperornis*, the creature was judged to be almost as old as *Archaeopteryx*, but while *Archaeopteryx* had feathered wings, *Hesperornis* lacked wings entirely, having instead of any kind of forelimb the vestiges of a humerus.

[6] Ibid., p. 14

[7] Ibid , Chapter 1 "Taking Wing," pp. 44 - 45; Chapter 6, p. 148

[8] Ibid., Chapter 6, p. 141

[9] Ibid , Chapter 1, p 23

[10] Ibid., p. 37

[11] Ibid., Chapter 6, pp. 141 - 142

[12] Ibid., p. 142

[13] Ibid , p. 144

[14] Ibid., p. 145

[15] Ibid., pp. 145 - 146

[16] Behe, Michael J , *Darwin's Black Box* (Simon & Schuster, 1996), Chapter 11 "Science, Philosophy, Religion," Section "History Lesson," p. 237

[17] Such an argument seems problematic when one considers that *Scientific American* (Vol 267, No. 1, July, 1992) published a review by Stephen Jay Gould of Phillip E. Johnson's *Darwin on Trial* ("Impeaching a Self-Appointed Judge," pp 118 - 121) but refused to allow Prof. Johnson to respond (*Darwinism Comes to America* [Harvard University Press, 1998] by Ronald L. Numbers, "Introduction: Darwinism, Creationism, and Intelligent Design," p. 17). Indeed, as Johnson himself points out in the second edition of his book *Darwin on Trial* (InverVarsity Press, Downers Grove, Illinois, 1993), *Scientific American* not only refused to allow him to respond, the editors refused to print any letters defending him ("Epilogue: the Book and Its Critics," p. 161). One would have thought courtesy, if nothing else, required the publication of at least one dissenting letter to so long and acerbic a review. Certainly when Melvin Konner wrote an unflattering review of Richard Dawkins' *Unweaving the Rainbow* for the March 1999 issue of *Scientific American*, the magazine did not hesitate in the letters section of is July issue that year to print a rejoinder by William P. Frost.

[18] He even wrote the Forward to *What is Creation Science* (Master Books, 1987) by Henry M. Morris and Gary E. Parker, a publication of the Institute of Creation Research. Here he suggests that the scientific community's disregard of creationist ideas is alien to the spirit of true scientific inquiry, and he suggests that scientific research into the question of origins is not truly opened but is conducted in service to a philosophical agenda I suggest, parroting the evolution biologist Richard Lewontin, that the philosophical agenda is an a prior commitment to materialism (*New York Review of Books*, January 9, 1997, p. 31)

[19] Meyer, Stephen C., "A Scopes Trial for the '90s", *The Wall Street Journal*, December 6, 1993, p. A14

[20] Pun, Pattle P T., *Evolution Nature and Scripture in Conflict?* (Zondervan Publishing House, Grand Rapids, Michigan, 1982), Part I "Scientific Bases of the Theory of Evolution," Chapter 1 "Historical Development of the Theory of Evolution," Section 3 "Mechanisms of Evolutionary Changes· Lamarckism vs Mendelism," p 33

[21] Numbers, Ronald L., *Darwinism Comes to America*, Chapter 1, Section "Evolutionary Theories," p. 33

[22] Ibid., p. 35

[23] Ibid., Section "Why Evolution?", p 43

[24] Pun, *Evolution Nature and Scripture in Conflict?*, Chapter 1, Section 4 "Classical Mutation Theory vs. Neo-Darwinian Evolution," p 45

[25] Numbers, *Darwinism Comes to America*, Section "Evolutionary Theories," pp. 35 - 36

[26] Pun, *Evolution Nature and Scripture in Conflict?*, Chapter 1, Section 4, p 45

[27] Gatewood, Willard B Jr. (editor), *Controversy in the Twenties* (Vanderbilt University Press, Nashville, 1969), Introduction, p 31

[28] The trial itself began on Friday, July 10, 1925, and lasted until Tuesday, July 21 Initially Clarence Darrow planned to called a variety of scientists as witnesses but on Friday, July 17, Judge John Raulston decided that although the scientists could submit their opinions to the court in writing, they would not be allowed to testify. The trial was over the following Tuesday so it is doubtful that the court had time to receive much less consider many of those opinions. Matt Ridley points out that in Ronald Fisher in Britain had in fact reconciled Darwin and Mendel in 1918 yet he also notes that the problem· Darwinism's demand for

variety and Mendelism's creation of stability, remained (*Genome*, Chapter 3 "History," p. 46)

[29] Patterson, Colin, *Evolution*, Biography, p viii

[30] Johnson, Phillip E., *Darwin on Trial*, Chapter 1 "The Legal Setting," pp 9 - 10

[31] Patterson, Colin, *Evolution*, Chapter 14, Section 5, p. 120 (right column) - p. 121 (left column)

[32] Ibid , p 122 (right column)

[33] For example in the 1989 edition of *The Selfish Gene* (Oxford University Press) on page 278 in the footnote to the phrase "... strategies and tricks of the living trade . " found on page 55 (Chapter 4 "The gene machine"), Richard Dawkins, whose feelings were apparently hurt by her critical review of *The Selfish Gene* published in *Philosophy*, sneers at her as "someone called Mary Midgley."

[34] Midgley, Mary, *Evolution as Religion* (Methuen and Company, New York, 1985), Chapter 2 "Do science and religion compete?", section "The Wilberforce legend," pp 10 - 11

[35] Dawkins, Richard, *The Blind Watchmaker* (W. W Norton & Company, New York, London, 1986), Chapter 9 "Puncturing punctuationism," p 225; Chapter 11 "Doomed rivals," p. 292

[36] Wilford, John Noble, "Dinosaur-era 'man tracks' were just a fundamental mistake," *Chicago Tribune* (Sunday, June 29, 1986), pp. 1 - 2

[37] It should be noted that mere variation within species is not, strictly speaking, proof that species can through natural means generate new species from within themselves. While evolutionists begin with inter-species variations and argue that evolution builds upon those, it should be noted that whether dark or light, peppered moths remained one species: *Biston betularia*.

[38] Wells, Jonathan, "Second Thoughts about Peppered Moths," *The Scientist* (May 24, 1999)

[39] I think here of Stephen Gould's complaint in the aforementioned review of Johnson's book that were direct observation and experiment the sole criteria for defining science, then all historical sciences "would disappear" (*Scientific American* [July 1992], "Impeaching a Self-Appointed Judge," p. 120). One can only scratch one's head in amazement at such hyperbole The disciplines would not disappear, they would simply lose their claim to be science They would

instead be reclassified. We have already moved in this direction by distinguishing between the "hard" and "soft" sciences.

[40] I wrote this paragraph in mid-1999 In 1969 a small creature was unearthed in Kyrgystan in Central Asia. Named *Longisquama*, it was stored in Moscow until the end of the millennium at which time it went on tour in the United States where John Rubin and Terry Jones, two Oregon State University paleontologists, saw it at a display in a Kansas shopping mall. The researchers classified *Longisquama* as an archosaur and placed it at the dawn of the Triassic Period 220 million years ago just as dinosaurs were beginning to proliferate and well before the appearance of *Archaeopteryx* 145 million years ago. What makes the creature pertinent to our discussion is that it had fully developed feathers and a skeleton that was very bird-like. How opened were theorists to this stunning addition to their data? Not very if Jacques Gauthier of Yale University is any indication. Confronted with the specimen, he made the remarkable observation that a theory with much supporting evidence cannot be toppled by a single exception. But of course a theory can if the exception is of sufficient import – as this one might prove to be.

[41] Dawkins, Richard, *Reweaving the Rainbow* (Houghton Mifflin Company, 1998), Preface, p. xii; Chapter 3 "Barcodes in the Stars," p 57

[42] Ibid., Chapter 11 "Reweaving the World," p 281

[43] Ibid., p. 274

[44] Ibid., Chapter 3, p. 50

[45] Gould, "Impeaching a Self-Appointed Judge," *Scientific American* (July, 1992), p 120

[46] Whitehead, Alfred North, *Science and the Modern World*, Chapter 12 "Religion and Science," p 183

[47] Colin Patterson makes this abundantly clear when he concludes *Evolution* by observing that the theory does contain a message about our relationship to the universe that is more positive than the message of the Old Testament that human beings are unique. Evolution, Patterson assures us, teaches us that humans are not unique, we are animals (Chapter 16 "Evolution and humanity," Section 5 "Human nature," p. 148, right column).

[48] Dawkins, Richard, *The Blind Watchmaker*, Chapter 1 "Explaining the very improbable," p. 6

[49] Popper, *Conjectures and Refutations*, Chapter 1, Section ii, p 38; Section vii, p. 50; Chapter 3, Section 2 "The Issue at Stake," p 102, Chapter 4 "Towards a Rational Theory of Tradition," pp. 127 - 128, 131

Appendix to Part I

The problem of classification

The problem of classification is subsidiary to the larger epistemological problem: how do we know a thing is what it is. As we saw in chapters one and two, the West, where epistemology has been the central problem of philosophy, initially solved that dilemma by supposing the existence of a realm of forms which not only gave structure to the world but made it intelligible. As the life sciences emerged, this supposition of a formal reality undergirded attempts to organize and classify the myriad sorts of living things with which the natural historian would deal. The Linnaean system devised in the eighteenth century assumed a realm of archetypes and attempted by comparing homologous structures among plants and animals to organize them around those archetypes. This became the basis of our system of binomial nomenclature which is used even today in the twenty-first century. Nevertheless, as we saw, there was a growing suspicion by Linnaeus himself that species might not be archetypal but might instead change within the parameters set by archetypes which might be expressed as more basic levels of classification like genera, or families, or orders, or wherever one chose to draw the line. Evolution theory, by exploiting the idea that change might be possible within the more immediate levels of classification like species, extrapolated the possibility of change at the more basic levels and so worked to undermine the Linnaean system. As the concept of species became increasingly problematic, the concepts which built upon the idea of species became unstable. Indeed, it was intrinsic to Darwinism itself that this should be so. Thus there was a conflict between Linnaeus and Darwin. On the one hand Darwin and his followers insisted that forms did not really exist and that life was malleable. On the other hand Linnaeus and his followers insisted that while species might change, it was plain that the more basic orders of classification did not. Species might form under the classification of genera, but new genera were not forming under the classification of families, nor new families under the classification of orders, and so forth.[1]

    We should notice that this disagreement between Darwin and Linnaeus is predicated upon two very different views of biology and classification. The Linnaean position develops from a classification system that is basically non-historical. The archetypes exist apart from the processes in which they are expressed. Indeed, it is they which make those processes intelligible. The Darwinian position is historical. It denies that archetypes exist, and devotes its full attention to the processes themselves. However, the Darwinian position must grapple with the problem of intelligibility in a way that the Linnaean position need not. After all, Linnaeus, when cataloging homologies, could appeal to archetypes to justify his system. The reality of the archetypes was illustrated by the homologies themselves. Darwin's followers could make no such appeal. For them concentrating on the processes meant that even the individual, which was itself in process, was relativized. Thus the Linnaean system was in jeopardy and there were no species to explain the origin of. Agassiz, as we saw, was well aware of this dilemma and appealed to it as a reason for rejecting Darwin. Darwin dismissed Agassiz's objection as a philosophical quibble, but it was not, precisely because the Darwinists took process so seriously.[2] After all, science seeks to systematize environments and to do that, it must generalize. But if process is supreme, how does one conceptualize it?[3]

Biological systematists have responded in two ways. There are those who argue that their role is simply to classify apart from any theoretical concerns. They see their goal in purely practical terms: to develop a catalog that will enable biologists to find species quickly. In opposition to these systematists is another group who insist that nothing is gained by constructing such a non-theoretical inventory. They argue that classification should be used to explicate principles that unify biology around a concept of natural law. Thus their purpose is preeminently theoretical.

In Germany in 1950 Willi Hennig, who was to become one of the leading proponents of this second group of systematists, published *Grundzuge einer Theorie der phylogenetischen Systematik* in which he attempted to establish a method of classification that mirrored the order of nature by stressing its relational aspects via a branching diagram or "cladogram."[4] The book, after extensive revision, was published in North America in 1966. It proved to be a watershed event in the history of systematic biology.

Hennig, defining science as "the systematic orientation of man in his environment,"[5] and appreciating the somewhat artificial distinction between structure and process, sought to erect a theory of systematics that would express as completely as possible the immanent, contingent, and historical nature biological organisms.[6]   To do this Hennig first recognized that individual organisms were the basic elements of biological systematics but that such individual organisms varied considerably among themselves and varied within their own developmental processes, a reality that made biological systematics extremely complicated.[7] Indeed, he pointed out that in metamorphosis the differences in the various stages could be so great that in some circumstances it was useless to attempt to classify the organisms by comparing their physiological characteristics.[8]   Thus Hennig proposed developing a system of classification that focused on the *semaphoront*, which he defined as an individual during a certain stage of development.[9] Hennig regarded the properties of a semaphoront as a multidimensional construct comprised of its physiological, psychological, and morphological characteristics, and he believed that in it he had discerned a biological element that related to living things rather than to properties of life or specific living processes.[10]   The semaphoront, he argued, and not the individual per se must be considered the basic element in systematics.[11]

Having established the unit upon which he wanted to build, Hennig critiqued two errors he believed misled other taxonomists. The first was the idea that science could proceed without   making assumptions.[12]   The second   was   the assumption that similarities themselves illustrate the primary relationships between individuals.[13]   He insisted instead that science proceeds precisely because it does make assumptions, that merely producing an accurate catalog of species, while a technical triumph, is not a scientific one,[14] and that similarity can be deceptive while dissimilarity can conceal relationships.[15]   For this reason phylogenetic systematics, as imagined by Hennig, purposes to explore genealogical relationships rather than simply comparing morphological semblance,[16] and to employ a model that is hierarchic since hierarchic systems best express the relationship of descent.[17]   Phylogenetic systematics, realizing that multiplicity within a historical framework is as much a characteristic of life as any other, and recognizing that this temporal dimension corresponds to the genetic one, purposes to use those insights in its investigation of life.[18] Its task is to determine the direction changes in characteristics took, to reconstruct their phylogeny, and by doing that to model the phylogenetic relations between species.[19] Thus he must determine how these various changes are integrated.[20]   His approach to this task, he argues, will be science and not art.[21]

As science, however, it can only be provisional.[22] Hennig then discusses several problems in identifying species, the most important one being their mutability. Species are impermanent,[23] and can maintain themselves only if they can in some way isolate themselves genetically.[24] Indeed life can be imagined as a stream.[25] The categories within this stream exist as a series of "interbreeding populations" that have a beginning and an end and are identifiable by the genetic connections that link their various developmental phases.[26] Such populations not only have a temporal dimension, they are also closely related to specific geological spaces.[27] Hennig then imagines his task as comparable to that of a map maker who must determine how fragments of a larger map are related to one another,[28] except in Hennig's case the map he must deal with is the map of time and the fragments of that map are the interbreeding populations or species. Of course it is not possible to observe genetic connections directly,[29] which means that in the end one must resort to "comparative holomorphology"[30] which he defines as "tak[ing] into account the body-bound characters of the individuals."[31] Thus we are back to the homologies of earlier classifications.[32]

But there are other problems as well. Because our observations are always bound to the present,[33] because the primary concern of systematics is organisms as bearers of characteristics (semaphoronts), and because it is not possible to determine genetic relationships directly, those relationships, which it is Hennig's purpose to investigate, must be determined by secondary means.[34] Such means are usually defined by taxonomic rules that were developed pragmatically, but the use of which can lead to false inferences since, variability being key to the process of evolution, one occasionally discovers exceptional cases where the rules do not apply.[35] Thus the artistic element, the element of insight, reasserts itself.[36] By claiming that his approach will transform systematics from an art to a science, Hennig is asserting a level of certainty for his method that, with its provisional quality and its reliance on secondary means, it cannot attain. For example, the attempt to establish an experimental systematics based on chemistry is in Hennig's mind predicated on a "gross logical error" since systematics determines relationships between ideal organisms while experimentation determines relationships based on the interaction of elements.[37] Furthermore, not all comparisons are equally instructive. Efforts to define relationships by comparing the parasites that infest various groups is complicated by the fact that, because of their stable environment, parasites tend to change much more slowly than their hosts,[38] and can only be employed for those groups connected to others by a host-parasite relationship.[39] It is also necessary that the absolute rank of one of the two members of a parasitic relationship be established by other means.[40] Even attempts to demonstrate phylogenetic relationships based on chromosomes, promising as they are, are complicated by phenomena like convergence, parallelism, or homoiologies.[41]

In paleontology the situation is even more complex. Hennig notes that since it can never been know precisely when species cleave, the systematist can never say for certain if fossil individuals from different time horizons belong to the same or to different species.[42] Also in classifying types, the paleontologist is dependent solely on morphological criteria that provides data that because it is far coarser than that provided by living species, enables the systematist to construct only coarse models.[43] He also notes that as the time horizons grow more distant and the life forms more alien, the less reliable our assumptions about those life forms become since our assumptions are informed by our immediate circumstances.[44] Thus the phylogenetic process that Hennig is proposing is not available to the paleontologist.[45] It fails in all groups incapable of fossilization and even fails to a considerable degree in groups where only superficial impressions of body parts are preserved.[46] It is also inapplicable to vast periods of earth's history and even where it can be used it is limited by the incompleteness of the record. Thus even by the most optimistic standards, the paleontological method can gauge only the minimal age, not the actual age, of a group.[47]

Hennig believes that, since evolution has become accepted, it is one of biology's most important tasks to determine the laws by which it works.[48] He also believes that phylogenetics, because it claims "that all evolution of taxonomic groups can be understood only as progressive differentiation"[49] and is thus so closely related to the concept of evolution,[50] can play an important role in that task, although it cannot provide a complete understanding of the evolutionary process and its laws.[51] Hennig claims this is so because the "grand strategy of evolution" is far vaster than any of the elementary processes that fuel it and therefore a knowledge of those processes alone is insufficient to unravel the larger picture of evolving life.[52]

There are several things to notice about Hennig's proposal. First, it is plain that he is struggling with the epistemological dilemma with which we began this study. Materialistic evolution or Darwinism, by abandoning appeals to formal reality, undercut the Linnaean system that had provided the framework for biology and left the science with no obvious philosophical justification for its systematization. Biologists could appeal to structuralism or conceptualism, conceive species as impositions of the human mind, and maintain that the classification system they were constructing was nothing more than a catalogue to help humans orient themselves in the world, but if science wishes to investigate the actual world beyond the human one, that position seems unsatisfying. In fact, when Plato proposed formal reality, his purpose was to integrate human thought with the world. By abandoning forms, scientists discovered they had alienated themselves from nature. As we wondered above, if process is supreme, how does one conceptualize it? Thus evolution created a great upheaval in biology, and one with which biologists still wrestle as they attempt to classify species and to orient themselves in the world of living beings. To abandon the idea would not destroy the science, as is so often claimed, but would reintegrate it with the world it wishes to investigate.

Second, Hennig addresses this problem by asserting the primacy of historicity or the temporal dimension of life and arguing that the division between structure and process is artificial. He then seeks to classify life forms using a hierarchic structure based on genealogical relationship or descent, but since such a relationship cannot be directly observed, he is forced to use morphology or homologies. Of course the system that results is provisional, but since science itself is provisional, Hennig does not see that as a problem. However, we contend that the phylogenetic systematics not only has much in common with art, but seems to employ a proleptic approach where one seeks to justify one's initial insights. Proleptic insight into morphologies is intended to track lines of descent into the distant past. But not all comparisons are equally instructive. As Shipman points out, if cladistic methods are applied inappropriately, the resulting cladogram is wrong.[53]   And, as Zimmer points out, in theory a dozen species can be arranged into millions of evolutionary trees.[54]   While chromosomal analysis may help eliminate many of these possibilities, it has its own complexities, as we saw above, and often gives results that make a hash of paleontological scenarios. After all paleontology is bound in what it can do by crude morphology often based on fragments of increasingly alien life forms.   It must confront extensive gaps in its evidence, and it can never know when species cleave. Chromosomal analysis may help to refine paleontological speculation and vice versa, but it is doubtful that the two even working in tandem will ever be definitive.

We should also note that chromosomal analysis is revealing that the transfer of genes among species appears to be far more common than anyone suspected. What impact this discovery will have on future evolutionary scenarios is not yet clear but at a minimum it would seem to emphasize the distinction between genotype and phenotype and to further tangle the evolutionary map.

However, there is another problem for cladistics to which Shipman refers. Cladistics assumes that anatomical characteristics held in common define a group. But that assumption is antievolutionary since, if such characteristics define a group, that group by definition has always had those characteristics. Thus, if one wishes to assert the reality of evolution, then shared characteristics, while they may help to identify members of a group, cannot actually define that group. But that assumption undermines the discipline of cladistics.[55] Thus evolution undermines Hennig as thoroughly as it undermined Linnaeus.

Hennig makes a host of assumptions, many of which were referred to above. But one of his most basic is the assumption that the present recapitulates the past. In once sense he must make such an assumption since biologists derive their principles from their study of present life forms. Thus, bound to the present, they must assume it is much like the past if they are to be able to unravel the mysteries of the past. Indeed, Hennig insists the rejection of the law of recapitulation is unjustified,[56] and employs Ernst Haeckel's now defunct phrase "ontogeny recapitulates phylogeny" when discussing the use of larval stages to assist the systematist in classifying insects.[57] But in fact we do not know that the past is recapitulated in the present. That is an assumption we make based in part upon necessity and in part because we make two other assumptions: the assumption of uniformitarianism borrowed from geology and the assumption that life is an expression of purely physical laws which we borrow from chemistry.[58]

We now surmise that a catastrophe at least on the scale of Noah's flood has occurred. What else would one call a meteor strike ending the age of the dinosaurs? And there is no way for us to know whether or not God authored such a catastrophe. Indeed, the Bible implies that he may well have (see Revelation 8:10 - 11). Thus catastrophism is again a viable option.[59] And there is no way of knowing whether life, especially consciously interacting animal life, is a purely chemical phenomena. Life of any sort has yet to be synthesized, but even if it were, its generation in a test tube would still prove nothing one way or the other about its ultimate genesis. The most one could say is that intelligent beings were able to contrive conditions where life under some definitions emerged. Frankly, God fits quite nicely into such an hypothesis.

In other words, the belief that the forces of geology and interactions of chemistry if given sufficient time can produce you reading this book I have written and that the two of us from our present perspective can grasp enough of the process to understand it remains a statement of faith.[60]

Endnotes

[1] In the 1940s, for example, L. Cuenot, F. von Huene, and R. Woltereck were arguing that no new "structural types" had developed for six hundred million years and that "cladic evolution" was over (Hennig, Willi, *Phylogenetic Systematics* (University of Illinois Press, 1979, translated by D. Dwight Davis and Rainer Zangerl), Chapter 3 "Problems, Tasks, and Methods of Phylogenitics," Section "Explosive Radiation, Typogenesis, and Related Concepts," p. 223).

[2] Indeed, the second chapter of *The Origin of Species* is a critique of the term species. In this chapter Darwin purposes to highlight the vagueness of the term for its imprecision is absolutely central to Darwin's thesis that individual differences are the foundations of varieties and that such varieties are "incipient species." See, too, his chapter on hybridism The problem for Darwin is not species vagueness but the fact that "species come to be tolerably well-defined objects," an issue he discusses in Chapter 6 "Difficulties on the Theory," pp. 148 - 150.

[3] Darwin in an effort to defuse this problem argued that the Linnaean system was in fact made more coherent by the proposition of descent from a common ancestor. He argued that the system was genealogical and illustrated pedigree Indeed, he compared the development of species to the development of language (Chapter 13, pp. 344 - 345) and even argued that rudimentary organs could be compared to letters retained in the spelling of a word but no longer used in its pronunciation (Chapter 13, p 372). Notice that Darwin's argument not only discovers a second example of evolution theory in the Bible (the tower of Babel story in Genesis), but is really no argument for evolution's truth. It is instead an effort to fit the theory into the preexisting model of classification.

[4] Hennig, concerned that neo-Darwinism allowed for a potentially limitless proliferation of theories of evolution, sought to establish an objective standard against which the probable accuracy of such theories could be measured.

Recognizing that the theories were predicated to some extent on observable relationships among organisms, Hennig, who imagined these relationships as a hierarchy, sought to express them in diagrams that would delineate as clearly as possible the extent of the evidence supporting the assumed relationships These diagrams of the hierarchical structure of relations between organisms are called cladograms. While the word, which comes from the Greek *clado* for branch, appears nowhere in Hennig's text, it does describe the approach to classification he adopted. He notes while contrasting the concepts of phylogenesis and evolution that "phylogenesis is intrinsically tied to the concept of species splitting and the consequences of this process" (*Phylogenetic Systematics*, Chapter 3, Section "The Concepts of Evolution and Phylogenesis," p. 198).

[5] Hennig, Willi, *Phylogenetic Systematics*, Chapter 1 "The Position of Systematics Among the Biological Sciences," Section "The General Concept of Systematics," p. 3

[6] Ibid., Section "The Special Tasks of Biological Systematics," p. 6 Note particularly Hennig's awareness of the conceptual relationship between the Darwin and Einstein and his concerns that biologists have not learned to fully exploit the new paradigm. Also note Chapter 2 "Tasks and Methods of Taxonomy," Section "Chorological Relationships for the Taxonomy of Lower Group Categories," where he defines species as "a complex of spatially distributed reproductive communities" and then observes that in this definition "it is necessary to extend the concept of space to the multidimensional environment" (p. 47. Clearly temporal sequence is for Hennig a fundamental aspect of this multidimensionality. See, too, page 66 in the Summary subsection to the Section "The Species Category in the time Dimension"). Hennig insists that since the diversity of living conditions fundamentally impacts the reproductive relations between individuals, it must be taken into account if one wishes to explain speciation (pp. 48 - 49). Life is "a multidimensional diversity" distributed across multidimensional environments (Chapter 1, Section "The Phylogenetic System and Its Position Among the Possible and Necessary Systems in Biology," p 24)

[7] Ibid., Chapter 1, Section "Special Tasks of Biological Systematics," p. 5

[8] Ibid., Chapter 2, Section "Comparative Kolomorphology as an Auxiliary Science of Taxonomy: the Allomorphism of Species," subsection "Metamorphism," p. 35; Section "The Delimitation of Higher Group Categories and the Determination of their Relative Rank and Order," p. 122

[9] Ibid, Chapter 1, Section "The Special Tasks of Biological Systematics," p 6 On page 65 in Chapter 2, Section "Species Category in the Time Dimension," subsection "Summary," Hennig writes, "The semaphoront (the character bearer)

must be regarded as the element of systematics because . we cannot work with elements that change with time."

[10] Ibid., p. 7

[11] Ibid., Section "The Phylogenetic System and Its Position Among the Possible and Necessary Systems in Biology," p. 12

[12] Ibid., p. 11. Hennig makes several assumptions. For example, he operates from the conviction that all correspondences and differences between species arose as characters in the original stem species [defined as the species from which two other species come - Chapter 1, Section "The Phylogenetic System and Its Position Among the Possible and Necessary Systems in Biology," p. 20] were altered and he is willing to make presumptions about the preconditions of these original characters (Chapter 2, Section "The Delimitation of Higher Group Categories and the Determination of their Relative Rank and Order," pp. 128 - 129).

[13] Ibid., p. 12

[14] Ibid , p 8 Hennig argues that it is not the accuracy of such a taxonomy but its theoretical underpinning that is useful to the biologist. Hence systematics purposes to investigate relationship between natural things with the purpose of discovering what laws are revealed in those relationships. Clearly for Hennig natural laws (or categories) are not something we impose upon nature (as they were for Kant) but something fundamental to nature and discoverable. Thus he insists species are not an "artificial invention" any more than are cells, though the practical difficulties in identifying species are considerably more daunting (Chapter 2, Section "Chorological Relationships of Individuals and Their Significance for the Taxonomy of Lower Group Categories," p. 52) According to Hennig, not only are species real, so are the higher level classifications expressed in the hierarchy of descent Indeed, their reality is secured by their basis in genetics and is there whether we recognize it or not (Chapter 2, Section "The Taxonomic Task in the Area of the Higher Group Categories," subsection "The Mode of Origin of Higher Taxa and the Question of Their Real Existence," pp. 79 - 81). However, Hennig points out that their reality means that our constructions of the relationships can be false. If we misidentify the genetic relationships within the hierarchy, our categorizations will be inaccurate (p. 83).

[15] Hennig makes this point in a variety of places, asserting very specifically, " ..there is no firm relationship between the degree of morphological similarity...of species and the degree of their phylogenetic relationship.. " (Chapter 2, Section "The Taxonomic Task in the Area of the Higher Group Categories," subsection "The Mode of Origin of Higher Taxa and the Question of Their Real Existence," p. 76).

[16] Hennig, *Phylogenetic Systematics*, Section "The Phylogenetic System and Its Position Among the Possible and Necessary Systems in Biology," p. 10

[17] Ibid , pp. 15 - 16

[18] Ibid., p. 26

[19] Ibid., Chapter 2, Section "The Delimitation of Higher Group Categories and the Determination of their relative Rank and Order," p 128

[20] Ibid., p. 129

[21] Ibid., [Prelude to Chapter 2], p. 28

[22] Ibid., p. 29. Hennig does not see this as a problem, of course, since he understands all science as provisional (p. 28).

[23] Ibid., Chapter 2, Section "Taxonomic Tasks in the Area of the Lower Categories," p 30

[24] Ibid , Section "Chorological Relationships of Individuals and Their Significance for the Taxonomy of Lower Group Categories," p. 51

[25] Ibid., Subsection "Summary," 65

[26] Ibid., Section "The Taxonomic Task in the Area of the Higher Group Categories," subsection "The Mode of Origin of Higher Taxa and the Question of Their Real Existence," p. 81

[27] Ibid., Section "The Delimitation of Higher Group Categories and the Determination of their relative Rank Order," p. 133. In Section "Chorological Relationships of Individuals and Their significance for the Taxonomy of Lower Group Categories," Hennig defined species as "a complex of spatially distributed reproductive communities." He calls this relationship in space "vicariance" (p. 47), a word he also uses to express the phenomenon of sister groups replacing one another in space (Section "Absolute Ranking of Higher Taxa," subsection "Measurement of Absolute Ages of Higher Taxa," p. 169). And Hennig stresses as beyond question the importance of the role played by geographical-spatial isolation in speciation (Chapter 3, Section "Phylogenesis and Space," p 230).

[28] Ibid., pp. 130 - 131

[29] Ibid., Section "Taxonomic Tasks in the Area of the Lower Categories," p. 31

[30] Ibid., p. 32

[31] Ibid., Section "Comparative Holomorphology as an Auxiliary Science of Taxonomy: the Allomorphism of Species: General," p. 33

[32] We defined homologies as traits which, though sharing similar locations and basic structures in various kinds of creatures, differ in form and function Hennig explicitly identifies homologies with the evolution process by asserting that they are to be regarded as transformation stages from an original character, and that transformation refers to the process of evolution and not to the possibility that the characters express formal derivations in a idealistic morphology. (Chapter 2, Section "The Delimitation of Higher Group Categories and the Determination of Their Relative Rank Order," p. 93)

[33] Hennig, *Phylogenetic Systematics*, Chapter 2,Section "The Species Category in the time Dimension," subsection "The Species Concept and Paleontology," p 64

[34] Ibid , Section Taxonomic Tasks in the Area of the Lower Categories," pp 30 - 31

[35] Ibid., Section "Comparative Holomorphology as an Auxiliary Science of Taxonomy: the Allomorphism of Species," p. 36

[36] Hennig justifies this by referring to a mathematician who might uncover or intuit a truth before being sure of the mathematical proof of that truth (Chapter 2, Section "The Delimitation of Higher Group Categories and the Determination of Their Relations in Rank Order," p. 129).

[37] Hennig, *Phylogenetic Systematics*, Chapter 2, Section "The Delimitation of Higher Group Categories and the Determination of Their Relations in Rank Order," pp 104 - 105. Hennig also questions whether the experimental method can be applied to phylogenesis (Chapter 3, Section "The Concepts of Evolution and Phylogenesis," p. 201), but argues that since experiments are intended to test suspected causal relationships that were first noticed through the comparative method (p. 202), and since the comparative method can also guide one's observations in phylogenesis, the differentiation between the two is not absolute, though he does recognize that the difference, based on the experimenter's ability to control the conditions of an experiment and to repeat an experiment, is real (p 203). Thus he argues that phylogenesis can be classed as a science.

[38] Ibid., p. 111

[39] Ibid., Section "Absolute Ranking of Higher Taxa," p. 174

[40] Ibid., p. 175

[41] Ibid., Section "The Delimitation of Higher Group Categories and the Determination of Their Relations in Rank Order," pp 115 - 118. Hennig defines homoiologies as distinct from homologies in the sense that, while they occur in narrow kinship groups, they develop independently in the bearers and are not found among close relatives (p. 117).

[42] Ibid., Section "The Species Category in the Time Dimension," subsection "The Species Concept in Paleontology," p 63

[43] Ibid, pp. 64 - 65; Section "The Delimitation of Higher Group Order Categories and the Determination of Their Relative Rank Order," p 140 This problem is complicated by the realization that the soft tissues are often reveal more about relationships between animals that the bony tissues reveal, but of course the soft tissues are not generally preserved Have paleontologists have are scraps of fossilized bone.

[44] Ibid., Section "The Delimitation of Higher Group Order Categories and the Determination of Their Relative Rank Order," pp. 140 - 141

[45] Ibid p. 140

[46] Ibid , Section "Absolute Ranking of Higher Taxa," subsection "Measurement of Absolute Ages of Higher Taxa," p 163

[47] Ibid

[48] Ibid., Chapter 3, "Problems, Tasks, and Methods of Phylogenetics," Section "The Concepts of Evolution of Phylogenesis," p 197

[49] Ibid , Section "Explosive Radiation, Typogenesis, and Related Concepts," p. 219

[50] Ibid., Section "The Concepts of Evolution of Phylogenesis," pp. 197 - 198

[51] Ibid., p 199

[52] Ibid , p. 200. Although the phrase "grand strategy of evolution" and the implication that it is greater than the sum of its parts is arresting, Hennig does not develop the concept further. Perhaps it was no more than a rhetorical flourish, but, if so, it was a very revealing one.

[53] Shipman, *Taking Wing*, Chapter 4, p. 107

[54] Zimmer, *At the Water's Edge*, Chapter 4 "Darwin's Saplings," p 98; Chapter 9, p. 218

[55] Shipman, *Taking Wing*, Chapter 9 "Dragons Fly," pp 213 - 214

[56] Hennig, *Phylogenetic Systematics*, Chapter 2, Section "The Distribution of Higher Group Categories and the Determination of Their Relative Rank and Order," p. 96

[57] Ibid., p. 122

[58] Since physical laws seem to be the same across the universe, and since to look into the universe is to look into the past, we may be confident that the same physical laws applied on the ancient earth as apply today It does not follow from that, however, that life developed in the past as it develops today. There may be a host of other factors impacting life, or some forms of life, that cannot be accounted for by physical laws.

[59] There is even growing evidence that the Genesis flood itself may be based on an actual event: the Mediterranean's breaching of the Bosporus strait and creating the Black Sea in 5600 BC. See *Noah's Flood* (Simon & Schuster, 1998) by William Ryan and Walter Pitman

[60] Notice too that the appeal to "sufficient time" makes the belief non-falsifiable and hence non-scientific. After all, if the interactions of geology and chemistry fail to produce you reading my book, one can always claim that it is only because insufficient time has elapsed.

Part II: Communication

Intent and comprehension intertwined
In signs by which mind reaches into mind.
These emblems of intelligence we find
In symbols: worlds constructed out of mind.

Mike Carter

Chapter 4

Communication as General Revelation

Introduction

There are multiple scenarios for every facet of the evolutionary process as it is currently imagined. The plausibility of any given scenario is dependent on its initial assumptions. That proposition, which should be self-evident, reminds us that evolution theory is system dependent. What is more, the scenarios indicate the flexibility of the paradigm itself, a flexibility that is consequent to evolution theory's character as more retrodictive than predictive.

 Traditionally science has attempted to verify its proposed principles by experiment. The experiments were intended to test predictions made based on hypotheses. If a given hypothesis was predictive, that hypothesis was considered verified. Such verified hypotheses could be formulated as principles, and the principles could be used to posit a model of the universe. Newton's theories, among the most rigorously tested in the history of science, are an example of how such model building works. The ideas which are elegant and predict with stunning accuracy became the building blocks of a model of the universe we now know was spectacularly wrong. The world as it appears to us is three dimensional, a box in which things move. The first chapter of Genesis describes how in the first three days God built a box and in the second three days filled it with moving things. Newton retained that box but made it infinite. Einstein did away with the box entirely. The universe as imagined today is curved, four dimensional, and finite. The exquisite predictability achieved by Newton was an insufficient basis for constructing a model of the cosmos.

 Unlike Newton, Darwin was more retrodictive. Basing his argument on present conditions, he attempted to project those conditions into the past, not to explain the present so much as to explain the past. Once the past was explained in terms of the present, the present appeared to make sense in terms of the past. This self-referential argument is known as uniformitarianism, and its primary method of explanation is story. We are story-telling animals, creatures who construct narratives to make events comprehensible in our terms. Stories are among the tools by which we humanize the universe, but for precisely that reason there is no reason to believe they are true in any absolute sense. At best we can say only that our stories are cultural expressions of the way we have organized certain types of data. They are our ways of answering questions we ask as we confront the great mystery. They are dim lights we shine into the darkness. And when our questions change, the stories change.

In this section I want to challenge evolution theory by asking a question about communication. And I will argue that given evolution's materialistic assumptions, communication as many if not most animals experience it should be impossible. But first we must understand that the word "communication" can be understood in several senses.

Communicate, communism, and community all share the same Latin root: *communis* meaning common. Communication involves a sharing where something peculiar is imparted and made common. This exchange requires a generalized connectedness that may be expressed in any number of ways. Inanimate objects like rooms can communicate with one another. Disease can be communicated between organisms, as can information. But in whatever form communication occurs, it is predicated on having something in common.

Like communication, the word "information" is also of Latin origin and suggests the internalization of a pattern in the Platonic sense. Hence, the communication of information between two organisms involves something abstract.[1] Signals and signs inform, although an obvious connection between the signal and the information it conveys is by no means necessary. For example, the way a dog holds its tail tells other dogs and me something about that dog's emotional and mental state. This ability to transmit information about emotional and mental states implies some level of community between dog and dog and between human and dog. For communication to occur between humans and dogs, we must be able to imagine to some degree what it is like to be a dog, and we may suppose that a dog in some way intuits what it is like to be a human. This ability to intuit secures the appropriateness of response and is based on empathy.

It is important to distinguish here between effect and response. While cause and effect may appear to be the same as stimulus and response, they are fundamentally different. An effect is invariable. A response is not. A response implies not effect but affect, a feeling or emotional state, or an imaginative construct upon which one acts. Response expresses inwardness, a disposition, an idea, or most generally a combination of these factors. When effective communication occurs at the information level, the signal of one being is accurately interpreted by another being and appropriately acted upon. Effective communication requires highly integrated patterns of stimulus and response.[2]

The question addressed here is: can genetics alone establish communicative common ground? This question is important for two reasons. First, it has evolutionary implications. The theory of evolution has always been a theory about relationships, relationships where shared qualities are assumed to be based on descent. Such qualities of relationship have always been recognized, even when applied to life forms. After all, Linnean taxonomy precedes evolutionary theory. But, in the case of life forms, they were thought, prior to Darwin, to express something essential in nature itself. For those who believed the doctrine that all was created by God, the similarities between different species revealed the hand of their Maker. As Francis Bacon put it, to study nature was to think the thoughts of God after him. But with Charles Darwin's *On the Origin of Species by Means of Natural Selection* (1859) all that changed. Rather than appealing to essentialism, evolution supposes that similarities between life forms are similarities of descent. Creatures resemble one another not because they express archetypes or reveal the mind of God but because they share a common ancestor. As Daniel Dennett pointed out in the early chapters of *Darwin's Dangerous Idea*, by appealing to kinship evolution does away with essentialism.[3] However, as we have just observed, the communication of affective states also suggests some level of commonality. If the theory of evolution understood as descent with modifications caused by random genetic changes cannot account for communication, we have reason to suppose the theory is false or at least inadequate. Second, since communication is such a widespread phenomenon, it may express something essential about fundamental reality and hence have something important to tell us about God.

A statement of the problem

Michael J. Behe, Associate Professor of Biochemistry at Lehigh University in Pennsylvania, has argued in *Darwin's Black Box* (The Free Press, New York, 1996) that the extraordinary complexity of those biochemical processes comprising a cell are compelling evidence for design and hence for a Designer. Pointing out that these processes resemble Rube Goldberg machines, Dr. Behe reasons that since they do nothing until all their components are fully in place, it is impossible to imagine how natural selection could have created them from simpler processes since effective simpler processes do not exist. He calls his argument the argument from irreducible complexity. I think his insight is a powerful one and I would like to apply it to communication phenomena. Mutations are autonomous but communication involves community. Hence, communication, like biochemistry, is irreducibly complex. Given such complexity, it is not easy to imagine how communication could be created contingently and via autonomous mutations.

This, it seems to me, is the crux of the problem: while we might imagine how a genetic mutation could change the behavior or appearance of an organism, it is not easy to imagine how such a change could provoke another organism to respond appropriately, yet such a condition-specific response is exactly what communication requires. It also follows that the difficulty in imagining how a genetic mutation could create both a change in one organism and a response to that change in another organism suggests that communication may transcend genetics.[4]

To illustrate: suppose a mutation in a butterfly caused it to perch on a branch and open and close its wings at regular intervals thereby sending a "signal" to others of its kind. Unless those others responded appropriately to this behavioral innovation (let us say they attempt to mate with the signaler), the "signal" would not be a signal at all, merely an non-productive waste of effort or worse be a "signal" to predators. We can imagine how randomness might generate unproductive effort but how can it generate productive response to what would otherwise be unproductive effort? Yet if evolution is true, such randomly generated communication must have been exceedingly common since communication itself is exceedingly common. Indeed communication is so common it would appear to express something fundamental to nature. That fundamental quality, I would argue, is community. Something in nature seems predisposed to organizing unrelated elements into meaningful patterns, and communication points starkly to the existence of that something.

Room for a soul

Life, complex, abundant and sexual, can exist without being aware and without communicating. This tells us that while life may be a prerequisite for awareness and communication, those abilities are not automatic consequences or expressions of life, even of complex life. Something more is required and at a minimum it would seem to be something connected with protein and the nervous system. This insight has inspired scientists like Tilly Edinger and Harry J. Jerison to attempt to trace the evolution of consciousness by measuring the endocranial casts or endocasts of fossilized animals and living species. Dr. Jerison writes, "[T]he mind and conscious experience [are] constructions of nervous systems to handle the overwhelming amount of information that they process. Intelligence ... is a measure of the capacity for such constructions."[5]   Believing that brain size provides a rough key to intelligence, Dr. Jerison proposes a three-tiered model for brain evolution in vertebrates. On the first tier are fish, amphibians and reptiles. Birds and mammals occupy the second, and the genus *Homo* stands on the third tier alone with dolphins. Having proposed such a scenario, however, what impresses Dr. Jerison, and what must impress his readers, is the very conservative nature of brain evolution. Major jumps in brain size have occurred only twice: once between reptiles and birds and mammals with mammals developing a neocortex birds lack, and once between mammals and humans and dolphins.[6]   Furthermore both of these jumps occurred quite late in the fossil record. The fossil evidence should cause us to wonder if intelligence (which Dr. Jerison understands as a measure of consciousness) really conveys significant survival benefits since it developed so slowly.

While the correlation between consciousness and neural tissue might seem self evident, there are those who doubt that the presence of brains, even fully developed human brains, are necessary signifiers of consciousness. The rationalists of the seventeenth century famously believed that animals were no more than robots, and today there are those who argue that consciousness is a recent cultural construct. One of the best known defenders of this position is Julian Jaynes of Princeton University who in *The Origin of Consciousness and the Breakdown of the Bicameral Mind* argues that civilization and literacy were developed by nonconscious beings whose volition came from a "god voice" (itself nonconscious) that had evolved in the right hemisphere of their cerebrums. He believes consciousness emerged only with a cultural crisis in the second millennium BC, a crisis that was exacerbated by the earlier invention of writing, but he does not think this change was global. He suggests instead that the appearance of consciousness was spontaneous, local, and uneven and that only recently has its triumph been secured. Indeed he supposes the conquistadors were able to so easily subdue Mesoamerican civilizations because the Amerindians who built those civilizations were little more than automatons.[7] Obviously Prof. Jaynes believes that consciousness conveys some survival benefits, but, as in the case of Dr. Jerison's theory, those benefits are not immediately obvious.   Certainly if Dr. Jaynes is right, only a tiny fragment of the world's protoplasm has ever achieved consciousness, and that achievement is uneven and, considered from a evolutionist's perspective, contemporary.   In other words, consciousness is something of an anomaly. We should not have expected evolution to have produced it.

Another aspect of communication which bears on the problem we are considering is our experience of self as being in some sense unified. It is the isolation of the single self which makes communication necessary and so marvelous, but what exactly is this self? Does it have objective or only subjective and in some sense illusory existence? Richard Dawkins has described biology as "the study of complicated things that give the appearance of having been designed for a purpose."[8] The operative word for Prof. Dawkins is of course appearance. His study and the philosophy he has embraced while conducting that study convince him that teleology is no more than appearance and that design and purpose are the outworking of randomness over vast periods of time. If it is possible for biological processes over time to produce organisms that appear to have been designed, is it also possible for them to produce a self that only appears to be unified?

Daniel Dennett believes it is.   He argues in *Consciousness Explained* that there is no Cartesian Theater where all information is integrated, that instead consciousness is the creation of subprocesses distributed throughout the brain that constantly produce Multiple Drafts of external events.   As William Calvin has described it, the self is a committee of nerve cells.[9] This insight rests upon the work of Santiago Ramon de Cajal who a century ago first realized that rather than being a continuous net, the brain was composed of discrete units.   To date experiments conducted to unravel the phenomenon of visual awareness have confirmed the expectations of Professors Dennett and Calvin. What we experience as unified vision seems to be the on-going product of four distinct, parallel systems, each concerned with different elements of vision and each communicating with the others through various cellular layers.[10]   As Dr. Semir Zeki points out, this strongly suggests that there is no central point for integrating information.[11]

What we have is a situation where current scientific speculation proposes neural processes that, though apparently unconnected, generate one's experience of unified vision and one's sense of being a unified self. The irony is that the door the researchers and theorists have opened leads directly to the room of the soul. Daniel Dennett for his part is very clear about this. He is forced to posit a soul but interprets it in mechanistic terms. It is, he says, the final result of the actions of millions of tiny robots. A "soul" is generated by them and ends when their action ceases.

Prof. Dennett spends so much time trying to explain away what he calls "the ghost in the machine" because recent scientific experiments have made that ghost so apparent.   The unthinkable has occurred. Science has in effect demonstrated the necessity of a soul.   What materialists like Daniel Dennett must do is explain that discovery away. Yet Prof. Dennett wrestles with questions he is never able to fully resolve. Why should unconscious robots create consciousness?   Why should independent processes lose themselves in an illusion of unity? And why does consciousness involve any sense of self at all?

Considered from an evolutionist's point of view life could have evolved successfully and never become conscious. After all, as we have seen, consciousness seems to have only limited survival value and may even be imagined as a very recent phenomenon.   Indeed, even the development of a nervous system proved no guarantee for the evolution of intelligence.   The brain, as Dr. Jerison has shown, is a very conservative organ. Yet consciousness beings who can communicate elements of that consciousness to other beings are everywhere. Indeed, communicative consciousness is so common most people assume it exists across the universe.   Such communicative unified consciousness is, I submit, the expression of soul. I also submit that rather than being the final result of the actions of millions of tiny robots, soul is the agent which integrates that action.   And finally I submit evolutionists have convincingly if unwittingly demonstrated how extremely unlikely the evolution of soul was.

The Instability Factor

Since Darwin evolution has generally been conceived as the outcome of adaptation to a local environment. Such local adaptations, Daniel Dennett tells us, are the sources of evolutionary progress.[12] Hence evolution has a deterministic and a random quality to which one can appeal to account for both the rich variety and the intricate order of life. Though evolution draws its raw material from random mutations, that randomness is shaped by the balance of nature, a balance implying that environmental stasis is the norm. This perceived stasis is one of the key components to evolution's deterministic side. It provides mutations with the stability necessary to establish themselves. In the Darwinian model competition among individuals of the same species was the primary engine behind the origin of species. Hence change was assumed to occur very slowly.

However, recent studies have suggested that environments are far more dynamic than the static "balance of nature" model suggests. Hence evolution, if it is occurring on the grand scale necessary to make the theory a viable alternative to creationism, must be reimagined to include factors that far transcend local environments. According to Richard Leakey and Roger Lewin in *The Sixth Extinction*, evolution is fueled not only by adaptations to local environments, but also (and more powerfully) by the internal dynamics of ecosystems that behave chaotically, and by history itself, a history, they point out, that is fundamentally contingent and can involve global catastrophes like collisions with massive comets as well as more local disasters like epidemics. In other words, what we see as stasis is ephemeral and emerges out of a far higher degree of randomness than has previously been appreciated. One of the consequences of this discovery is that evolution is essentially unpredictable, placing it outside the realm of traditional science. A second consequence, and one that is for the moment of more interest to us, is how this randomness impacts community and communication.

Michael Behe's irreducible complexity argument is two pronged. First, it makes the point that the molecules and chemical reactions of life are not only tremendously complicated, they cannot be simplified and still be effective. Hence, it is not easy to imagine how they could have evolved from more simple processes. Second, one would assume from their complexity that the evolution of such processes, if it did occur, would require vast amounts of time. This second point is what the new picture of chaotic or dynamic nature subverts.[13] Instead of incremental development, the fossil record indicates that new forms of life appear suddenly during periods of instability and then maintain themselves relatively unchanged during periods of stability. The implication is that rather than breaking down orderly arrangements, instability is inexplicably the source of new expressions of order and that these forms appear quickly.

It seems to me that in the origins debate between essentialism and descent, the evidence as we have it today strongly favors the essentialist side. Order, even in its highly complex forms, would seem to be a fundamental rather than a contingent element to the universe, otherwise disorder would not be the vector of new and complex patterns of order. And of course essentialism, associated as it is with ontological universals, is the philosophical handmaid of natural theology.[14] As we saw in Chapter Two, so clearly has chaos theory established the essentialist position that James Gleick claims the reality of final cause is firmly established by Darwinism. And if Darwinism plus chaos theory have reintroduced Aristotle, we should note that Plato, too, has won reconsideration among mathematicians and logicians. Roger Penrose identifies Kurt Godel, the Austrian mathematician whose theorem demonstrated the centrality of intuition in mathematics, as "a very strong Platonist."[15] And Penrose himself believes that mathematical truth transcends algorithms and that consciousness is essential if only to judge which algorithm is generating true statements.[16] He writes, "I believe ... that our *consciousness* is a crucial ingredient in our comprehension of mathematical truth."[17] Interestingly he makes this claim only two pages after referring to the teleological dimension of evolution.

The evolution of language

We referred earlier to the conservative nature of brain evolution. The cost of having a brain is one explanation for that conservatism. As noted above, complex sexual life can generate abundance without benefit of a nervous system. Adding a nervous system conveys an absolute cost without absolute guarantees. If the cost is low enough, relative guarantees may compensate for it, but the biological cost of nervous tissue is high. The high cost of maintaining that nervous system coupled with its relative and diminishing returns explains the conservative nature of brain evolution.

Let us apply this insight to the current scenario proposed for human evolution and what it suggests about the evolution of language. I will borrow heavily here from the scenario sketched in Daniel Dennett's *Consciousness Explained* since he attempts to deal with the problem from a purely Darwinian standpoint.

Dennett begins with the proposition that considered genetically chimpanzees are our closest kin. He then argues from both genetic and fossil evidence that our line and that of the chimpanzee diverged approximately six million years ago. Two-and-a-half million years later our ancestors stood erect. While this change in posture had no appreciable effect on the size of our ancestors' brains, we can imagine that it left their hands free thus increasing the potential for tool manipulation. Another million years elapsed. Then in something over two million years our ancestors' brains swelled to their current size. Amazingly Dennett for theoretical reasons believes that this increase in brain size was not accompanied by language development, cooking (implying no real mastery of fire), agriculture, or any of those things we associate with higher intelligence.[18] It seems to have been an increase in potential, nothing more. From a Darwinian standpoint this scenario introduces a huge problem: what was the value at the time of this extraordinary advance? What forces selected for this unprecedented increase in potential?

To drive the point home, consider what Dr. Sherwin Nuland says concerning the human brain, its size and complexity, and the cost it imposes on the body. Dr. Nuland begins by pointing out that much of the structure of the human brain with its ten billion neurons and sixty trillion synapses is unique to our species.[19] He then writes:

> Though three pounds [the weight of the brain] represents a mere 2 percent of the body weight of a 150-pound person, the quartful of brain is so metabolically active that it uses 20 percent of the oxygen we take in through our lungs...Fully 15 percent of the of the blood propelled into the aorta with each concentration of the left ventricle is transported directly to the brain.[20]

In other words, Darwinists like Daniel Dennett expect us to believe that the human brain which is four times larger than the brain of a chimpanzee, which puts tremendous metabolic demands on the body, and which is vastly intricate and unique to our species, evolved in a little more than two million years from an ape's brain, an ape's brain which had served quite adequately for three-and-a-half million years and still serves our nearest genetic relatives quite well. How random natural selection could have accomplished so wonderful a feat when the huge, hungry, and unique brains offered no obvious survival value, Prof. Dennett boldly leaves to our imagination. Once this evolution was completed about 150,000 years ago nothing else happened for over a thousand generations until our ancestors discovered how to control fire, then evolved some kind of language, and finally about ten or fifteen thousand years ago began to domesticate animals and plants.

In the middle of this century Susanne Langer, a Whiteheadean who was also interested in the origin of language and consciousness, pointed out that language is universal among human groups and that even among those which have what she calls "the simplest of the practical arts," there are no archaic languages. All are fully and complexly present.[21]   She also suggests that language developed rapidly as members of our sociable species began to use sounds to name objects,[22] a scenario reminiscent of the second chapter of Genesis. Both she and Daniel Dennett believe for theoretical reasons that before language ability could develop, all the mental equipment had to be in place. Current science supports their surmise. Antonio R. Damasio and Hanna Damasio, a husband and wife research team at the University of Iowa, write that the evolution of language seems to have occurred after human or their progenitors had evolved the ability to categorize, and they go on to suggest that this process is recapitulated in infant development.[23] The point, that conceptualization preceded the evolution of language, makes sense. Before speaking, one should have ideas to express. But this also suggests that language as we know it is neurologically distinct from communication per se since the purpose of language is precisely the accurate communication of complex concepts.   Indeed, the model proposed by the Damasios is profoundly teleological and leaves us wondering how the three interacting sets of neural structures which the Damasios believe process language in the brain could evolved through natural selection.

Conclusion

It is time to summarize our points and draw our conclusions. First, we have suggested that the commonness of communication implies community as a fundamental reality in nature. Second, we have also suggested that at least theoretically community and communication may be more basic than consciousness and that consciousness itself might be a construct of community, either a community of interacting neural structures or of human culture. Third, we have pointed out that brain evolution as revealed in the fossil record seems to have been very conservative, a phenomena which casts doubt on the selective advantage not only of intelligence but more particularly of higher intelligence. Fourth, we have posited communication as an example of irreducible complexity and hence as something that probably did not evolve from simpler processes. Having described communication as an example of irreducible complexity, we have attempted to distinguish between simple communication and human language and have stressed the teleological implications in the origins of human language. And fifth, we have argued that irreducible complexity along with a new awareness of the chaotic dimensions of nature and an increased appreciation of the role of intuition in mathematics point to essentialism rather than kinship as a more viable explanatory paradigm of origins.

The world as it appears today is not the world Darwin and his nineteenth century champions would have anticipated. It is a world where life evidences far more variety than would have probably occurred through descent with modification. It is also a world where natural systems are far more chaotic than Darwin, convinced by Charles Lyell's uniformitarianism, was willing to allow. It is a world where order and community are generated in the midst of these chaotic systems, a world where knowledge is predicated on intuition and empathy, a world where community and intuition together make communication possible, a world which requires soul. Hence, it is a world made more intelligible by essentialism than by inheritance, and a world which appears far more likely to have been fashioned by a purposeful creator than to have evolved randomly out of chaos. Finally as the artifact of a creator, it is a world which reveals things about its creator. I believe that communication as an example of irreducible complexity is revelatory.

What would communication as an example of irreducible complexity tell us about a Designer/Creator? It would tell us that community and communication might be an essential aspect of that Designer/Creator.

How might community and communication as an essential aspect of a Designer/Creator impact our creation dogma? Many religions lack an adequate doctrine of creation. Hinduism and Buddhism, for example, posit life's purpose as an escape from illusion and a return to Brahma or Nirvana but leave opened the question of why the original illusion was generated or expressed. Judaism and Islam (see Sura XIII) offer a solution to the mystery of creation by assuming creation glorifies God, but they leave open the question of why a perfect monotheistic deity would choose to create, or why, having   created,   he   would   make himself   available   to   his creation.   Christianity solves this problem. Like Judaism and Islam, Christianity supposes that God is glorified and revealed through His creation, but, unlike Judaism and Islam, Christianity via the doctrine of the Trinity makes such a glorification comprehensible. By presenting God as essentially .communal and loving, Christianity unveils creation as a natural outflow of God's communal love. And since God's love is the highest love, our glorification of God becomes a communication in love and rebounds to our benefit. Of course this communication is secured for us by the sacrifice of Christ who via his Holy Spirit draws us into communication with God. As Andrew Murray observed:

> When the Father gave the Son a place next to Himself as His equal and His counselor, He opened a way for prayer and its influence into the very inmost life of Deity itself.[24]

Finally, the Christian doctrine of the Trinity offers an explanation for why communication is so common. Communication in creation is rooted in communication within the Godhead, and creation, spoken into existence by God, is an icon of the mind of God. As John tells us:

> In the beginning was the Word, and the Word was with God, and the Word was God.

Endnotes

[1] Organisms is a significant word here. The communication of information between computers is more like the communication of a disease. Nothing abstract is shared. Instead "bits" common to one machine are transferred to another

[2] It is of interest to note that efforts to respond to the problem presented here have tended to deny the distinction between cause and effect and stimulus and response. Thus communication as I mean it is imagined as a type of cause and effect. If that is all communication is, then my question is answered and my objection fails, for the issue I am raising is predicated on the assumption that cause and effect and stimulus and response express qualitatively distinct types of

interactions and that one could not have given rise to the other. The difference between the two illustrates the proposition that insensible matter could not have given rise to consciousness. There are two very different though interrelated realities at work here. My position of course is dualistic.

[3] This emphasis on relationship makes evolution a fundamentally historical theory, hence an aside by a historian might be of interest here In historical research relatedness though important is insufficient to establish connection For example, cultural parallels, many of them striking, have convinced some archeologists that there must have been significant pre-Columbian contact between the New and Old Worlds Detailed similarities between the forms and decorations of the pottery of the Valdivia culture on the northern shore of Guayas Province in Peru and the early Middle Jomon culture in southern Japan imply some connection between these people though how such contact may have been secured two-and-a-half millennia before the birth of Christ remains an open question (For a discussion of such similarities and what they imply see *Prehistoric Man in the New World* edited by Jesse D Jennings and Edward Norbeck [The University of Chicago Press, 1964], particularly the essays by Robert Wauchope "Southern Mesoamerica" and Alfred Kidder II "South American High Cultures".) In the same way, John W Emmert's 1889 discovery at Bat Cave on the Little Tennessee River of a small piece of light-tan sitlstone inscribed with letters bearing a striking resemblance to a type of paleo-Hebrew used in the first and second centuries AD have occasioned some speculation that there might have been a connection between the Woodland-period mound builders of central North America and the Jews of Roman occupied Palestine. (See *Biblical Archaeology Review* July/August 1993, Volume 19, No, 4, "Did Judean Refugees Escape to Tennessee?" by J Huston McCullogh and "Let's Be Serious About the Bat Creek Stone" by P Kyle McCarter, Jr) But most scholars dismiss such suggestions as simply too implausible to be taken very seriously. Similarities even when remarkable must be weighted against a host of other factors

[4] To the best of my knowledge Darwin never addressed this problem as such, but he was aware that what he called "correlated modifications" could present a difficulty for his theory. He addressed the issue in his discussion of the existence of sterile worker ants and resolved it to his satisfaction by noting that natural selection works on families as well as individuals (*The Origin of Species*, Chapter 7 "Instinct," p. 196) However, Darwin knew nothing of the laws of genetics Those laws underline the primacy of the individual in passing traits across generations. Such atomism undermines the stimulus/response necessary for the appearance of something like communication.

[5] Jerison, Harry J., *Evolution of the Brain and Intelligence* (Academic Press, New York and London, 1973), Part I "The Approach", Chapter 1 "Brain, Behavior, and Evolution of Mind", p. 4

[6] I should point out that Richard Leakey and Roger Lewin in *The Sixth Extinction* (Doubleday, New York, 1995) read Jerison as adding a third leap driven by the competition between ungulates and carnivores and occurring about sixty-five million years ago (Chap. 6 "*Homo sapiens*, the Pinnacle of Evolution?", p 95). Jerison discusses this in Part IV "Progressive Evolution of the Brain", Chap 13 "Progressive Tertiary Evolution. Ungulates and Carnivores" in *Evolution of the Brain and Intelligence* but in my opinion does not give it the same weight as the other three Of this advance he writes· "The progressive evolution of the brain can almost be characterized by a single word, 'diversification.' ... [T]he brain evolved in a way appropriate to behavior within a particular niche   But the brain did not evolve in an exuberant way. It has been a 'conservative' organ " (p 318) Indeed, the conservative nature of brain evolution *is* the problem.

[7] Jaynes, Julian, *The Origin of Consciousness in the Breakdown of the Bicameral Mind* (Houghton Mifflin, Boston, 1976), Book Two "The Witness of History", Chapter 1 "Gods, Graves, and Idols" He says: "The unsuspicious meekness of the surrender has long been the most fascinating problem of the European invasion of America. . It is possible that it was one of the few confrontations between subjective and bicameral minds. . . Not subjectively conscious, unable to deceive or to narratize the deception of others, the Inca and his lords were captured like helpless automatons. And as its people mechanically watched, this shipload of subjective men stripped the gold. ", p 160

[8] Dawkins, *The Blind Watchmaker*, Chapter 1, p 1

[9] Calvin, William H., *The River that Flows Uphill* (Macmillan Publishing Company, New York, 1986), Day 6, p 160

[10] Zeki, Semir, "The Visual Image in Mind and Brain", *Scientific American*, September 1992, pp 72 - 73

[11] Crick, Francis, and Koch, Christof, "The Problem of Consciousness", *Scientific American*, September 1992, p. 158

[12] Dennett, Daniel C , *Darwin's Dangerous Idea* (Simon & Schuster, 1995), Part II "Darwinian Thinking in Biology", Chap. 10 "Bully for Brontosaurus", p. 308

[13] Leakey and Lewin in *The Sixth Extinction* use the terms dynamic and chaotic interchangeably, basing the meaning of those terms on chaos theory

[14] For a very brief statement to this effect see Michael H Macdonald's article "Essence" (pp 365-366) in *Evangelical Dictionary of Theology* (Baker Book House, 1984), Walter A Elwell, Editor.

[15] Penrose, Roger, *The Emperor's New Mind* (Penguin Books, 1989), Chap 4 "Truth, proof, and insight", p. 113

[16] Ibid , Chap 10 "Where lies the physics of mind?", p. 412

[17] Ibid., p 418

[18] Dennett, *Consciousness Explained*, Part II "An Empirical Theory of the Mind", Chap 7 "The Evolution of Consciousness", pp 189-190

[19] Nuland, Sherwin B., *The Wisdom of the Body*, Chap 12 "Mining the Mind the Brain and Human Nature", p. 327

[20] Ibid., p 328

[21] Langer, Susanne, *Philosophy in a New Key* (Mentor Books, New York, 1951), Chap. 5, p. 99

[22] Ibid , pp. 118-120

[23] Damasio, Antonio R and Hanna, "Brain and Language", *Scientific American*, September 1992, p 89

[24] Murray, Andrew, *With Christ in the School of Prayer* (Whitaker House, Springdale, Pennsylvania, 1981), Chapter 17 "Praying in Harmony with God," p 128

Chapter 5

Communication: a Phenomenon Beyond Time

Introduction

Michel Foucault has observed that without the ability to generalize, communication would be impossible.[1] Language is possible, he says, because it exists on a foundation of "continuities, resemblances, repetitions, and natural criss-crossings."[2] This is true so far as it goes, but I would argue that communication, even at its most basic levels, involves our ability to *recognize* such "continuities, resemblances, repetitions" and the like. Communication, if it involves sharing abstractions between individuals, as most animal communication does, is an activity of consciousness and is fundamentally intuitive. Intuition itself is a form of generalization and as such is rooted in something transcending the immediate particular. My thesis is that this "something" is an uncreated reality that is more fundamental than created space/time, that it is in fact the inner-communication of the Trinity.

In this chapter I will discuss two very different theories of communication: one based on process philosophy and the other based on the recently popular discipline of memetics. I have chosen these because I believe their evolutionary emphasis underlines for us that non-temporal quality necessary for communication.

Process philosophy

In discussing process philosophy I will be relying on Stephen Franklin's *Speaking From the Depths*. I have chosen Franklin's book for three reasons. First, I studied under Franklin and therefore find his interpretation of Whitehead more accessible than I find the interpretations provided by other Whiteheadian scholars. Second, as an evangelical Franklin makes a serious effort to explicate process thought within an evangelical framework. Third, Franklin in *Speaking From the Depths* has addressed some of the same issues that I wish to address.

The notion of concrescence is central to process thinking. Roughly analogous to becoming, concrescence is the way actual entities emerge into the present as they prehend past actual entities.[3] For the purposes of analysis Whitehead breaks concrescence into phases, modifying their number according to his explicative purposes. Franklin, for his part, chooses to divide concrescence into five phases: the conformal phase, the conceptual phase, the comparative phase, the intellectual phase, and the satisfaction.[4] However, because these phases are somewhat discretional, Franklin reminds his readers that no actual entity need pass through them all, and that the fourth phase, the intellectual one, is often bypassed.[5]

The conformal phase is the phase of simple physical feelings.[6] In the conformal phase, the concrescing actual entity is comprised of past actual entities and is partially determinate and partially indeterminate.[7] It is determinate because it must conform to the past (hence the term conformal phase) but is indeterminate insofar as it has yet to achieve satisfaction and enjoys some freedom in determining how it will proceed to that end.   By the time it reaches satisfaction, it has prehended "in a perfectly determinate way every item in its universe"[8] and sustains no further changes.[9] Instead it becomes a datum for the next concrescence. Thus concrescence is the vehicle through which "the many become one experience, the satisfaction."[10] Note that datum which have achieved satisfaction are changeless, a condition they share with eternal objects. However, unlike eternal objects, they are not analogous to Platonic forms. Instead they represent the frozen and repeating past reenacted in each present moment, giving coherence to concrescence, and providing identity to the future. Through them cyclical time is incorporated into linear history.

In the conceptual phase or stage, abstract feelings emerge. These feelings have as their data eternal objects.[11] An eternal object is a "pure potential" for the characterization or determination of fact.[12] They may be imagined as Platonic forms.[13] Thus, the feelings associated with the second phase of concrescence do not emerge randomly. Instead they are conceptual prehensions derived from the physical feelings of the first or conformal phase.[14] Franklin points out toward the end of his book that since concrescence is the vital core of each actual entity, it must involve notions of ideals and values.[15]

In the comparative phase conceptual prehensions and physical feelings are integrated,[16] and the order latent in the first phase begins to surface.[17] This emergence of order occurs in conjunction with the appearance of physical purposes out of which evolve propositional prehensions.[18] These propositional prehensions can themselves be divided into perceptive feelings and imaginative feelings.[19] A perceptive feeling, the simpler of the two, is that feeling of contrast between the way an eternal object is felt and the way an actual entity is felt.[20] Thus perceptive feelings may be authentic or inauthentic.[21] An imaginative feeling distinguishes between eternal objects focused on a specific set of actual entities and the physical prehension through which those actual entities entered the concrescence. As such, imaginative feelings share much with inauthentic feelings.[22] The contrasts between authentic perceptive feelings, inauthentic perceptive feelings, and imaginative feelings are the stuff of propositions. Though Whitehead calls propositions "lures for feelings," Franklin is quick to point out that not every prehension of a proposition involves consciousness, but because they introduce potentially into a concrescing actual entity they have the power to evoke feeling.[23]

If consciousness is to emerge in a concrescence, it will do so during the fourth or <u>intellectual phase</u>. This is because consciousness is comprised of two types of intellectual feelings that are founded upon propositional prehensions. These two types of intellectual feelings are conscious perceptions and intuitive judgments.[24] Indeed, we are told that consciousness lurks in the subjective forms of these intellectual feelings, that it comprises both perception and intuition, and that the contrast between a proposition and the actual entities comprising its logical subjects, that is the contrast between theory and fact, or between what might be and what is, or between potentially and actuality, has of itself the power to create consciousness [25]

There are three things to notice before we move on. First, concrescence is felt. The entire process is characterized by feelings, whether physical or abstract, authentic, inauthentic, or imaginative. Indeed, as concrescence is central to the emergence of an actual entity, so feeling is central to concrescence. Since the ability to feel would seem to be a fundamental indicator of consciousness, this might suggest that consciousness is latent in all becoming, but that does not seem to be what is meant, and this brings us to our second point: a distinction is maintained between feeling and consciousness. All actual entities from a photon, to a star, to a block of granite, to a galaxy concress, but not all actual entities attain to consciousness. Third, consciousness enters into subjective feelings only when the actual entity has the power to contrast the imaginative with the actual. We might ask, whence this power? And we might also ask, does the ability to contrast what is real with what is potential suggest the presence of consciousness, or at least proto-consciousness?

Of course, Franklin does not hesitate to associate consciousness with the brain,[26] but on a more fundamental level he and Whitehead associate it with the soul.[27]   When discussing perceptions in presentational immediacy that occur without significant guidance from a conscious source and those that are guided by such a source (i.e. advanced percipients), we read that advanced percipients constitute a portion of the soul.[28] The soul is defined as a "[t]hread of conscious entities"[29] or as "a thread of actual entities, probably dwelling for the most part in the interstices of [a person's] brain."[30] During concrescence, these conscious actual entities comprising a soul thread must create the "work-a-day world" from the manifold Reality present in the first · stage of concrescence.[31] But because very few if any of the actual entities constituting a soul thread endure even for a second,[32] it follows that the unity of self we experience as sustained consciousness within that "work-a-day world" is dependent on an agent other than the soul thread. That agent is language. As the actual entities of a soul thread concress, language "elicits and promotes" selected propositions, making them available to consciousness and producing "the real potentiality which is a prerequisite to consciousness."[33] Thus mature human consciousness is not possible without language, and "the ability to deliberate…is a gift of language."[34]   Human thought, Franklin writes, that is thought characterized by "sustained consciousness and articulated memory," is dependent on language.[35]

An important distinction is assumed here between linguistic and nonlinguistic consciousness. Franklin argues that whereas an animal may be acutely aware of its immediate environment, it does not take its past experiences into account nor does it considered the future.[36] However, Franklin also points out that ideas precede language. If language is a form of symbolism, it must have ideas to symbolize. Hence we have thoughts, and struggle to find the right words to express them.[37] Franklin writes, "[W]e know and experience more than we can ever put into words…"[38] Thus the distinction Franklin wants to maintain between linguistic and nonlinguistic consciousness seems somewhat arbitrary. Communication certainly occurs between animals, and between animals and humans, suggesting animals can on some level entertain ideas similar to ours. They can also feel and act with intention. It seems more accurate then to say that consciousness is subjectivity and that language or animal signals are its way of objectifying its awareness for the interpretation of other consciousness entities. It would follow that feeling, not thought, is the fundamental witness to consciousness, and that conscious purpose or intentionality is born of feeling. The psychotherapist Rollo May argues that intentionality underlies will and decision,[39] and is the primary way we experience our identity.[40] He understands feeling as fundamental to both, and, not incidentally, he, too, appeals to Whitehead, through Susanne (he spells it Susan) Langer.[41]

Thus it is either wrong or very misleading to cast feeling in some non-conscious role as Franklin does. It would not even be accurate to portray feeling as preconscious. We assert instead that feeling is the fundamental witness to consciousness and that this can explain why animals are generally considered to be conscious beings despite their apparent inability to contrast theory with fact or potentiality with actuality. After all, animals give every indication of being able to feel and to possess intuition. But what is felt, and what is doing the feeling? We have argued that consciousness is subjectivity. Let us return to Franklin with this in mind.

To achieve satisfaction, an actual entity must simplify the infinite complexity that characterizes the initial phase of its concrescence.[42] Simplification is achieved through transmutation, the integrative process in the second or conceptual phase of a concrescence whereby the eternal object felt physically at the first or conformal phase is applied to the nexus of the prehending actual entity so that the nexus can be felt as though it were a genuine element in the world.[43] In this way the abstract feelings of the second phase are organized and emerge. Thus transmutation is the master principle of order,[44] or the master key to simplification.[45] It is also the necessary first step in the appearance of human consciousness since Whitehead indicates that, in humans at least, transmuted feelings are the ones which attain to consciousness.[46] Language aids humans in this process by helping us to simplify our experience as we search for the right word, and by directing our attention towards the units of experience we identify verbally.[47]

Franklin maintains that a propositional prehension has two aspects, its subjective form and the proposition itself, and he identifies the subjective form in a propositional prehension as an eternal object.[48] Recall that propositional prehensions emerge in the third or comparative phase of concrescence as conceptual prehensions and physical feelings are integrated. Recall, too, that consciousness, if it is to appear, emerges in the subsequent intellectual phase and lurks in the subjective forms of conscious perceptions and intuitive judgments, and recall that both of these are founded upon propositional feelings. Franklin observes that propositional prehensions have a noncognitive element introduced by the subjective form,[49] and that language "since it elicits the *prehensions* of propositions," also has its noncognitive side.[50] But, as he has also pointed out, such prehensions have the power to evoke feeling and, when organized by language, may become the foundation of that which is cognitive.   It would seem then that Franklin is suggesting that consciousness is a potential of certain eternal objects (recall that eternal objects are the data of abstract feelings as those feelings emerge in the second or conceptual stage).   Therefore, it would seem that if consciousness really is subjectivity, then in Whitehead's model as explicated by Franklin, consciousness *really is latent in all becoming*, and it would seem that there is something eternal about it. It winks on in certain momentary actual entities as those entities feel the contrast between what might be and what is, and it is clarified and unified by language. Either the contrast between potentiality and actuality has the power to generate a soul spontaneously, or it has the power to make the latent soul apparent. We assert that the later possibility is the more coherent.

　　　　We further assert that, given the assumptions of a process model, those conscious perceptions and the intuitive judgments that characterize the fourth or intellectual phase are ultimately creations of the non-temporal precisely because they have their source in eternal objects and in the prehension of data which are themselves changeless. And we assert that, though both conscious perceptions and intuitive judgments share a temporal side, (conscious perceptions are, after all, perceptions of conditioned entities, and intuitive judgments are rendered about those conditioned entities), the non-temporal element is especially pronounced in intuitive judgments. Not only then does the soul lie latent in all becoming, when it is actualized, it emerges out of the eternal.[51] It is not our purpose here to critique the orthodoxy of such a position, it is simply our purpose to show that in process thought consciousness is dependent on communication and is rooted in the eternal, that conscious communication must in some way take place beyond time, and that this non-temporality is an especially important aspect of intuition. If this sounds rather Platonic, it is helpful to recall that Franklin has reminded us early on that eternal objects can be imagined as Platonic forms and that he has specifically identified the subjective form of a propositional prehension as an eternal object.

Memes

In 1976 Richard Dawkins, at the conclusion of *The Selfish Gene*, proposed the existence of a new replicator: the meme. He wrote:

> [A] new kind of replicator has recently emerged on this very planet. .
>
> The new soup is the soup of human culture. We need a name for the new replicator, a noun that conveys the idea of a unit of cultural transmission, or a unit of *imitation* 'Mimeme' comes from a suitable Greek root, but I want a monosyllable that sounds a bit like 'gene ' I hope my classicist friends will forgive me if I abbreviate it to *meme* It should be pronounced to rhyme with 'cream.'[52]

In 1981 Edward O. Wilson and Charles Lumsden in the introduction to their book *Genes, Mind, and Culture* (Harvard University Press) proposed a rival word 'culturgen' which they defined as "the basic unit of inheritance in culture evolution."[53] But meme, being shorter and catchier, was the word that established itself and was eventually added to the *Oxford English Dictionary*. Indeed, meme has become the focus of a new field of investigation: memetics, a discipline that purports to investigate "the competition between memes to get into human brains and be passed on again."[54] There is even an online *Journal of Memetics*. The success of the word meme has led Richard Dawkins to protest:

> [M]y designs on human culture were modest almost to the vanishing point. ... My purpose was to cut the gene down to size, rather than to sculpt a grand theory of human culture.[55]

But such is the power of memes that, whatever Dawkins' intentions, a "grand theory of human culture" is precisely what he founded. Indeed, in the hands of some philosophers and psychologists, the meme has become a vehicle for investigating the origins of consciousness itself. Daniel Dennett is perhaps the best known of the philosophers who have explored the possibilities of the meme as an agent of consciousness. In *Consciousness Explained* he argues that consciousness is an illusion created as the brain, which acts as a massive parallel processing computer, produces multiple drafts of events out of which emerges the virtual reality which we experience as an integrated whole with us at its center and to which we react. Dennett posits consciousness as a kind of behavior generated as the neuron-based program is run, and he treats memes as self replicating ideas that are key to this process. As I have discussed Dennett's views elsewhere,[56] I will in this paper concentrate on Susan Blackmore's related proposal as it appears in her recent *The Meme Machine*. The book has enjoyed major media attention and Dawkins himself wrote its introduction.[57]

Prof. Blackmore is a Senior Lecturer in Psychology at the University of the West of England in Bristol. She researched the book during a long convalescence. Blackmore has no doubt that we, like all other life on this planet, evolved by Darwinian natural selection, yet she notes that we differ markedly from other animals (we have a disproportionately large brain, we have language) and she wishes to know why.[58] To account, within a Darwinian framework, for our uniqueness, she proposes two memetic theories, two processes, one of which she calls "meme-gene coevolution" and the other which she calls "memetic driving."[59]

Two stipulations underlie both these theories: Dawkins' supposition that memes, like genes, are replicators, and Dennett's argument that both can be conceived as algorithms. Blackmore interprets evolution as an algorithmic process, "a mindless procedure which when followed must produce an outcome."[60] She notes that algorithms are "substrate neutral"[61] and "must always produce the same result if they start from the same point."[62] She then notes that chaotic systems, being extremely sensitive to initial conditions, can, consequent to seemingly inconsequential differences in initial conditions, generate seemingly unrelated outcomes, and she observes that many natural systems are chaotic. Thus, she argues, algorithms coupled with chaotic systems are natural vectors for complexity.[63] Evolution, based on replicating entities, whether genes or memes, is an algorithm that, within natural chaotic systems, has spawned the tremendous diversity that characterizes living systems, whether those systems are biological or cultural.

Having argued that the intricate interconnectedness of the myriad systems that characterize the cosmos can be generated solely by mindless algorithms operating in a chaotic milieu, Blackmore proposes her two theories. First, she argues that memes and genes coevolved as "memes changed the environment in which genes were selected and so forced them to provide better and better meme-spreading apparatus."[64] Language is the example she uses to illustrate this idea. Language development, she reasons, was predicated on our ability to learn by imitation, an ability which, she argues, is very rare among animals and makes us special.[65] (It is worth pointing out that since she earlier defined memes as "whatever is passed on by imitation," a definition she derives from Dawkins' proposal that memes are passed on by imitation,[66] it is almost tautological for her to maintain that imitation facilitated the spread of memes. Consequently her conclusion is embedded in her premise.)[67] As language emerged memetic and genetic selection re-enforced one another with memes taking the principal role.[68]   Again she follows Dawkins who is also sympathetic to the proposition that language emerged gradually.[69] Language, she writes, with its complex grammatical structure was built upon simpler structures, a progression that was "the natural result of memetic selection."[70]   She notes that brains are "expensive to run," "expensive to build," and "dangerous to produce,"[71] and observes that its development "certainly looks like a runaway phenomenon."[72] Thus she argues that genes alone would not have evolved a large brain.[73] Instead its evolution is explicable memetically. She writes, "[T]he massive increase in brain size [was] initiated and driven by memes."[74] "[T]he human brain is an example of memes forcing genes to build better and better meme-spreading devices."[75] Language was not made possible by the appearance of a large brain and a vocalization system, rather language, once it appeared, restructured "the human brain and vocal system for its own propagation."[76]

This capacity for memes to create an environment that enables genes to create physical structures conducive to "high fidelity, high fecundity, and longevity,"[77] is what is meant by memetic driving. She writes:

> Memetic driving works like this. Once imitation arose three new processes could begin First memetic selection (that is the survival of some memes at the expense of others) Second, genetic selection for the ability to imitate the new memes (the best imitators or the best imitators have higher reproductive success). Third, genetic selection for mating with the best imitators [78]

Thus memes are "mind tools" that enable us to think,[79] they are also the tools through which better minds are built. It is of interest that although Dawkins has ridiculed as "preposterous" Whitehead's oft quoted remark that Western philosophy is a footnote to Plato,[80] he appeals to Plato when discussing the "self-normalizing ... error correcting" function of memes.[81] Plainly memes with such properties would resist change and as such would be vehicles of generalization.

Indeed, there is something dualistic in the division of reality into genetic and memetic parts. Dawkins, for example, does not understand Darwinism as a random process. Instead he insists that "survival of the fittest" derives from "a more general law of *survival of the stable*."[82] The evolution of life is the evolution of DNA, and DNA introduces stability into the world.[83] Indeed he argues that this stability is the source of the living complexity biologists seek to explain, a complexity he insists "embodies the very antithesis of chance."[84] The mutations that supply the evolutionary process with its raw material may occur randomly, but natural selection, the method by which they are shifted and winnowed, "is the very opposite of random."[85] He writes, "[M]ost of natural selection is concerned with preventing evolutionary change rather than with driving it."[86] And he points out that DNA is a replicator of such unparalleled fidelity that after five million replication generations only one percent of the units within the double helix may be miscopied.[87] Indeed, so impressed is Dawkins with the stability of DNA that he concludes *The Blind Watchmaker* with a rhetorical flourish that would warm the heart of many a creationist.

> The essence of life is statistical improbability on a colossal scale Whatever is the explanation for life, therefore, it cannot be chance The true explanation for the existence of life must embody the very antithesis of chance   The antithesis of chance is nonrandom survival...[88]

Like the actual entities of process thought, DNA's stability is reminiscent of cyclical time. Through DNA the history of a living organism is recreated in each mitosis, and coherence between the generations is preserved. Memes, as we have pointed out, are analogous to Platonic forms.[89] In the world as conceived by Dawkins, Dennett, and Blackmore, we are created as memes and genes interact.

Susan Blackmore, by associating human brains with genes and human minds with memes, reveals that she is well aware of the latent dualism in the genetic/memetic paradigm, and attempts to resolve what she understands as a serious problem by adopting a view not unlike the one championed by Daniel Dennett: she identifies dualism with consciousness, then denies that consciousness has anything to do with decision or creativity.[90] She concludes that each human being is a memeplex (a complex of memes), or a set of memeplexes, supported in a physical system, the body or meme machine.[91] One of the memeplexes that comprise this set she designates as a selfplex which is "a bunch of memes,"[92] "a fluid and ever-changing group of memes."[93] "Each selfplex," she writes, "gives rise to ordinary human consciousness based on the false idea that there is someone inside who is in charge."[94] And if a meme can become incorporated into a selfplex, that is, become associated with a person's self concept, that meme will be able to protect itself by encouraging behavior that works for its own propagation.[95] The selfplex makes no decisions, it simply propagates memes.[96] Thus the lives we live are based on a lie. There is no I who has opinions, no self who believes, there is only the illusion of selfhood, an "I" infected by memes which use that "I" to replicate themselves. We do what we do because memes make us do it.[97] She writes, "The self is not the initiator of actions, it does not 'have' consciousness, and it does not 'do' the deliberating."[98] Unsurprisingly she denies we have free will. Unsurprisingly she emphasizes that consciousness, by which she means subjectivity, "cannot *do* anything."[99]

I will point out that the dualism which concerns Dr. Blackmore has nothing to do with consciousness per se and everything to do with memes and genes. Therefore, her effort to reduce consciousness to illusion and thereby escape "the dualist trap" is an obvious diversion in her argument and fails to extract her from her dilemma. Whether we are conscious entities or not, the dualism remains because the dualism rests not on our consciousness but on the gene/meme dichotomy. However, it is not my purpose to critique Dr. Blackmore's conclusions here. Instead I want to focus on her assumption about communication. She is interested in humans so concentrates on language. Therefore, in discussing her position, we will also stress language. However, the point we wish to make involves not only language but any kind of symbol.

Susan Blackmore argues that talking is the vehicle by which memes spread.[100] To propagate themselves, our memes impel us to talk.[101] Our very capacity for language has been driven by memes, and its function is meme dissemination.[102] Indeed, both our brains and our language serve primarily as meme spreading vehicles.[103] They illustrate how memetic evolution can drive genetic evolution.[104] Remember that we are fluid memeplexes existing for a short period of time while memes themselves endure as trans-temporal entities. We, as Dawkins points out, are only temporary vehicles for a transitory combination of genes.[105] As such we are particular and unique, conditions that should render communication impossible for us. What makes it possible are the abiding memes. Indeed, for Blackmore, that is what communication is: the temporary incarnation of that which is abstract and potentially eternal: the meme.

Conclusion

We saw how in process thought conscious perceptions and intuitive judgments, the intellectual feelings elicited and promoted by language, are based upon the prehensions of actual entities and eternal objects that are changeless and hence non-temporal. We pointed out that these changeless non-temporal qualities made eternal objects analogous to Platonic forms and made actual entities comparable to cyclical time. Thus process thought, though opened to novelty, prehends moment by moment the changeless entities of an immutable past. And, as Franklin has shown, process thought builds its theory of communication and knowledge on the assumption that such eternal truths exist. For these reasons we contend that in process thought these changeless realities and eternal truths, which plainly derive from the Platonic tradition, make possible the kind of generalization Foucault recognized as necessary for communication.

In memetics we saw that replicators like memes are also reminiscent of Platonic Forms. They constitute the behaviors, ideas, convictions, and beliefs we hold as our own. Their ability to replicate as they are transmitted from mind to mind makes them potentially eternal, and it is their transmission from mind to mind that we call communication. Significantly memetics has its origins in Dawkins' reflections on evolutionary biology. There we saw that replicators like genes are analogous to cyclical time. That kind brings forth after its kind reflects the remarkable stability of DNA. The ancients recognized this phenomenon and reasonably linked it to seasonal patterns. Lacking our sense of historical depth, they imagined that such cycles repeated eternally.

We have argued that consciousness/subjectivity is initially evidenced not by thought but by sensation or feeling. It is at this level that mind first begins to organize world. Thus sensation precedes and transcends response and, it seems to me, constitutes a fundamental mystery: by what agency does a collection of molecules feel? Yet feeling is the basis of abstract communication since feeling gives rise to intuition and intuition is the foundation for higher level abstraction. If these abstractions are to be communicated, they must be generalizable, that is they must possess certain qualities that can be recognized or "felt" by more than one individual. This generalizability can be modeled as Platonic Forms, as the eternal objects of process thought, or as memes. How this generalizability is conceived is not important to our argument. What is important is that we recognize it as the basis of communication via symbols.

Now let us consider the Trinity. We begin by noting that our classic Trinitarian formula was constructed using Neoplatonic philosophical tools. In the New Testament (first century) Yahweh disappears into the philosopher's *theos*. John's identification of Christ as *logos* was interpreted within a substance/form paradigm by apologists like Justin Martyr (second century) to enable Christian theologians to distinguish between the Father and the Son. Subsequently, theologians like Irenaeus (late second century) used this insight to assert the unity of Father, Son, and Spirit in creation and redemption by arguing that God is an immutable, eternal being manifesting as divine reason (the Son) and divine wisdom (the Spirit). This tradition allowed Tertullian (late second and early third century) to argue that the Father, Son, and Spirit were of one substance and that the sonship of the *logos* began in his primal generation for creation, a model he christened as *trinitas* (English: trinity). However, it also enabled theologians like Clement of Alexandria (late second and early third century) to develop models of God very like the neo-Platonist triad (One, Mind, and World Soul), or for Origen (late second to mid-third century), Clement's successor, to argue that the Father is absolutely God while the Son's divinity, though no less real, is derivative, an archetype (or Form) of God but standing below God in a divine hierarchy. Spurred by Arius (third to fourth century) who would then argue that Christ was a creation and not God, the church at the Council of Nicea in the fourth century developed a trinitarian formula which identified the Son as *homoousios*,[106] (of one substance) with the Father, and as uniquely begotten by the Father rather than being made by him. This creed was the first to obligate the entire postapostolic church to a single theological declaration.

In the creed, identity is established in three ways. First, it is established substantially: *logos* and *theos* are the same because they share the same substance. Second, it is established relationally: *logos* and *theos* are the same because, unlike other entities, *logos* was not created by but was begotten by *theos*. Finally, identify is established functionally: *logos* is *theos* because *logos* functions as *theos*, *logos* creates and judges creation.

Neoplatonic influence on Cappadocian theology as formulated at the Council of Constantinople in 381 was even more obvious. Of the six cannons presented by the Council, the first is of interest to us. That canon upheld the Nicean Creed by affirming that the Godhead exists in three *hypostases* or modes, each mode sharing the same divine nature. Though there is no subordination among the three, the Father is nevertheless seen as somehow being the source of the Son and the Spirit. To explain how this might be possible, the Cappadocians employed an analogy based on *ousia* (substance) and *hypostasis* (mode). Each *hypostasis* is distinguished by specific characteristics but all share the same substance: they are *homoousios*.

It is important to remember here that each *hypostasis* is understood as a person, otherwise· terms like Father and Son make no sense. And these persons are understood to be in loving communion with one another. Thus Augustine could describe the Trinity as three persons united because they shared equally of the same substance, and mutually related in their love for one another. Such love is eternal, uncreated, intimate, and communicated. It would follow then that communication as an aspect of the Godhead is a reality more fundamental than creations like space/time.

Communication reflects the inner life of the Trinity. Hence communication, to be possible, must rely on generalizations that transcend time. This is why Plato was forced to posit a formal reality, and why even in process or evolutionary scenarios, though they ascribe the highest priority to the temporal side of existence, communication is assumed to be based on the sharing of transtemporal entities.

We are not *homoousios* with God. We will not be reabsorbed into the Godhead. We were created as distinct individuals and our individuality will be preserved. Not only that, those of us who are believers will be preserved in loving communion with the Trinity. We will share in an intimate communication that is more fundamental than creation itself.

Endnotes

[1] Foucault, Michel, *The Order of Things* (Random House, 1970), Part I, Chapter 4 "Speaking," Section VII "The Quadrilateral of Language," pp. 119 - 120

[2] Ibid , p. 120.   These natural criss-crossings he identifies as "a system of identities and differences .. manifested by the network of *names*." [Italics in the original]

[3] An actual entity is anything that exists, whether in the present or the past, that attained to full being but that in some measure had the potential to be different In other words, the being expressed by actual entities is conditional They are the things of the real world: its ponds, pebbles, and people, that are but did not have to be as they are. This potential to have been different than they are means that they are to be distinguished from eternal objects (a shade of green, for example) which are givens and do not change

[4] Franklin, Stephen T., *Speaking From the Depths* (William B. Eerdmans Publishing Company, Grand Rapids, Michigan, 1990), Part Four: Propositions, Chapter 1 "The Stages of Concrescence as the Context for Propositional and Intellectual Feelings," p. 2

[5] Ibid., Section IV, footnote 27 where he substitutes the word stage for phase, p 27

[6] Ibid , Chapter 1, Section 1, p 3

[7] Ibid , Chapter 2 "The Nature of Concrescence," Section I, subsection D, p. 42

[8] Ibid , Chapter 1, Section V, pp 29 - 30

[9] Ibid , Chapter 3 "Objectification and Actuality Whitehead's Protest against the Bifurcation of Nature," Section II, subsection D, p. 72

[10] Ibid., Chapter 2, Section I, subsection D, p 42 [Franklin quoting Whitehead]

[11] Ibid , Chapter 1, Section II, p. 3

[12] Ibid , p 4

[13] Ibid , Chapter 3, Section II, subsection C, p. 68

[14] Ibid., Chapter 1, Section II, p. 3

[15] Ibid., Part Four: Religion, Chapter 18 "Religious Experience," Section II, subsection B, p 310

[16] Ibid , Part One, Chapter 1, Section III, p 7

[17] Ibid , subsection A, p 9

[18] Ibid , subsection B, p. 9

[19] Ibid , p. 10

[20] Ibid.

[21] Ibid., p. 12

[22] Ibid , p 13

[23] Ibid , subsection C, p 17. We might wonder whence this power if there are no latent feelings to evoke

[24] Ibid , Section IV, p 27

[25] Ibid., pp 28 - 29

[26] Ibid., Chapter 5 "The Indicative System, the Locus, and Patterns," Section III, p. 114; Chapter 9 "Strain Loci," Section IV, p 177

[27] In Part Four, Chapter 19 "God and Religion," Section IV, subsection A, footnote 15, page 343, Franklin points out in passing that Whitehead considered Descartes' posited body/soul dichotomy incoherent. It would be interesting to know why, since Whitehead himself is very much a dualist, but Franklin never explains his statement. One supposes Whitehead considered Descartes' proposal incoherent because it resulted in the very bifurcation of nature that Whitehead himself strove to overcome as he developed his philosophical stance

[28] Ibid , Part Two Symbolism, Chapter 10 "Presentational Immediacy," Section IV, p. 194

[29] Ibid , Part Three Language, Chapter 12 "A Metaphysical Description of Language," Section III, p. 233

[30] Ibid , Section IV, p. 234

[31] Ibid , Chapter 17 "Some Concluding Observations," Section I, p. 297

[32] Ibid., Chapter 12, Section IV, p 236

[33] Ibid Section VI, subsection A, p. 245 Franklin points out on page 244 of this subsection that Whitehead has several names for propositions including "theories," "lures for feeling," and "tales which might perhaps be told about particular actualities "

[34] Ibid , p 246

[35] Ibid , Section VII, p. 253. One imagines that articulated anything would be dependent on language.

[36] Ibid , p Section IV, subsection A, p. 246. He never tells us how he knows this

[37] Ibid., Section VII, p. 253

[38] Ibid , Chapter 14 "Language and Abstraction," Section II, p 268

[39] May, Rollo, *Love and Will* (W. W. Norton & Company, Inc , New York, 1969), Part II "Will," Chapter 7 "The Will in Crisis," p, 201

[40] Ibid , Chapter 9 "Intentionality," p 243

[41] Ibid., Part III "Love and Will," Chapter 12 "The Meaning of Care," pp 303 - 304

[42] Franklin, *Speaking From the Depths*, Part One, Chapter 13, Section IV, p 261, Chapter 14 "Language and Abstraction," Section II, p. 268

[43] Ibid., Part One, Chapter 1, Section III, subsection A, pp. 7 - 8

[44] Ibid., p 9

[45] Ibid , Part Three, Chapter 13, Section IV, p 262

[46] Ibid

[47] Ibid., Chapter 14, Section II, p 268 - 269

[48] Ibid., Chapter 13, Section III, p. 259

[49] Ibid., Part Four, Chapter 20 "The Language of Religion," Section III, subsection B, p 366

[50] Ibid , p. 367. Italics in the original.

[51] It seems fairly clear that if feeling rather than thought is the better indicator of consciousness, then one could hardly claim that consciousness is latent in concrescence. Instead consciousness is very much a part of the process, and its presence is indicated initially by physical and abstract feelings. Indeed, it seems to me that the very possibility of imaginative and inauthentic feelings in the

comparative phase would require the presence of consciousness and intuitive judgment, suggesting that the simplification achieved by transmutation requires consciousness.

[52] Dawkins, Richard, *The Selfish Gene* (Oxford University Press, 1989 [new edition]), Chapter 1 "Memes, the new replicators," p. 192

[53] Blackmore, Susan, *The Meme Machine* (Oxford University Press, 1999), Chapter 3 "The Evolution of Culture," Section "Sociobiology and culture on a leash," p. 33

[54] Ibid , Chapter 1 "Strange Creatures," Section: "Meme fear," p. 9

[55] Dawkins, *The Selfish Gene*, Endnotes to Chapter 11, pp. 322 - 333

[56] See *Perspectives on Science and Christian Faith*, Vol 51, No 2 (6/99) "Consciousness Explained?"

[57] For example, *Time* in its April 19, 1999, issue reproduced part of Richard Dawkins' introduction as an article under its "Ideas" section (pp. 52 - 53) This is accompanied by an Unmesh Kher essay outlining some of the position staked out in the controversy Susan Blackmore's book is sure to ignite·

[58] Blackmore, Susan, *The Meme Machine*, Chapter 1 "Strange Creatures," p 1

[59] Ibid , Chapter 9 "The limits of sociobiology," p 108. In *Unweaving the Rainbow* (Houghton Mifflin Company, 1998), Dawkins defines coevolution (unlike Blackmore, he hyphenates the word) as "the evolving together of different organisms ., or between different parts of the same organism " (Chapter 12 "The Balloon of the Mind," p 289) Plainly Blackmore is thinking in terms of the latter meaning

[60] Ibid., Chapter 2 "Universal Darwinism," Section "The evolutionary algorithm," p 11

[61] Ibid She observes, "The substrate does not matter – only the logic of the procedure does "

[62] Ibid., p 12

[63] Ibid

[64] Ibid., Chapter 8 "Meme-gene coevolution," p 93

[65] Ibid., Chapter 1, Section "What makes us different?," pp 3 - 4; Chapter 4 "Taking the meme's eye view," p 50. On page 49 she states, "Imitation is learning something about the form of behaviour through observing others, while social learning is learning about the environment through observing others," a distinction she attributes to a 1993 article "Imitation, culture and cognition," that appeared in *Animal Behaviour*

[66] Ibid., Chapter 4, section "Not everything is a meme," p. 43; Section "Imitation, contagion, and social learning," pp. 51 - 52 Dawkins, when he first proposed the idea, argued that memes spread by imitation (*The Selfish Gene*, Chapter 11, pp 192, 194) and has defended that definition consistently For example in *Unweaving the Rainbow*, Chapter 12, p 302, he writes, "A meme is. anything that replicates itself from brain to brain, via any available means of copying," then broadens that definition somewhat a couple of pages later by defining a meme as "[a]nything that spreads by imitation " (p 304)

[67] In correspondence with me, Blackmore admits the tautology but says, "I was only trying to spell this out clearly for those who might otherwise miss the importance of imitation arising in early humans."

[68] Blackmore, *The Meme Machine*, Chapter 8, Section "Language spreads memes," p 99

[69] Dawkins, *Unweaving the Rainbow*, Chapter 12, p 195

[70] Blackmore, *The Meme Machine*, Chapter 8, Section "Language spreads memes," p 104

[71] Ibid , Chapter 6 "The big brain," Section "Origins of the human brain," pp. 70 - 71

[72] Ibid , Section "Did memes drive brain size?", p 79

[73] I made a very similar argument in "Consciousness Explained?", my critique of Dennett's position, so I was gratified to see Susan Blackmore discuss this problem

[74] Ibid , p. 75

[75] Ibid , Chapter 9 "The limits of sociobiology," Section "Memetic drive and Dennett's tower," p. 119

[76] Ibid., Chapter 8, p. 104

[77] Ibid   Such qualities would be prerequisites for any successful replicator, a point Dawkins raised early (*The Selfish Gene*, Chapter 2 "The Replicators," p 17) and which Blackmore reiterates (Chapter 8, p 100, Chapter 5 "Three problems with memes, Section "We do not know the mechanism for copying and storing memes," p. 58)

[78] Ibid., Chapter 9, Section "Memetic drive and Dennett's tower," p. 116

[79] Ibid., Chapter 18 "Out of the meme race," Section "Human foresight," p 240

[80] Dawkins, Richard, *Unweaving the Rainbow*, Chapter 8 "Huge Cloudy Symbols of a High Romance," p 193

[81] Blackmore, *The Meme Machine*, Forward by Richard Dawkins, p. xii

[82] Dawkins, *The Selfish Gene*, Chapter 2, p. 12

[83] Ibid , p 16

[84] Ibid , *The Blind Watchmaker* (W W Norton & Company, 1996), Preface, p xv

[85] Ibid , Chapter 2 "Good design," p 41

[86] Ibid , Chapter 5 "The power and the archives," p 125

[87] Ibid

[88] Ibid., Chapter 11 "Doomed rivals," p 317

[89] In correspondence with me Blackmore objects to the identification of memes with Platonic forms   She writes: "[M]emes are not like Platonic Forms at all Plato thought these forms existed independently of any instantiation Memes are not like this. They are behaviours that are copied If there is no behaviour or no instructions for building the behaviour, then the meme disappears forever " Her point is technically true but I do not believe that in raising it she really addresses the problem I do not claim that Platonic Forms and memes are a perfect or even a near fit. I claim only that they are analogous, that they share a similar function Dawkins himself notes this in the forward to her book as I point out above

[90] Blackmore, *The Meme Machine*, Chapter 16 "Into the Internet," Section "Writing," p 207   However, she explicitly differs from Dennett by rejecting his view the illusion of self is benign (Chapter 17, Section "Where am I?", p 225, Chapter 18, Section "Free will," p. 237   She writes, "[L]iving a lie cannot be

morally superior to accepting the truth." (Chapter 18, Section "The ultimate rebellion," p 245)

[91] Ibid., Chapter 18 "Out of the meme race," pp 235 - 236. In correspondence with me Blackmore objects to this statement writing: " [Y]ou say 'she concludes that each human being is a memeplex' I don't think I have ever said that What I mean to say is that the self is a memeplex A human being is a body, brain and memes." For the sake of the reader I will quote what Blackmore says on page 235 "Each of us is a massive memeplex running on the physical machinery of a human body and brain − a meme machine " I am not sure I see where the problem with my statement lies If each of us is not a human being, what are we?

[92] Ibid , Chapter 17 "The ultimate memeplex," Section "The selfplex," p. 231

[93] Ibid., Chapter 18, Section "Human foresight," p. 241

[94] Ibid , p 236

[95] Ibid , Chapter 17, Section "The selfplex," p 232

[96] Ibid Chapter 18, Section "The ultimate rebellion," p. 245

[97] Ibid., Chapter 17, Section "The selfplex," pp 233 - 234. This use of the word "infect" is interesting Recall that in footnote 1 of chapter 4 I pointed out that information sharing between computers is more like the transfer of a disease than it is like the communication of abstractions, a form of communication that I argue is based on intuition. Applying the infection metaphor to memes suggests that what we experience as intuition is on closer examination similar to information sharing between computers But the use of such a metaphor obscures far more than it illumines After all, memes are only signals that the mind uses to create information, they are not information per se. Also, comparing intuition to infection sidesteps the issue of our experience, the great mystery of awareness itself Information transfer based on intuition requires awareness while communication based on an infection metaphor does not

[98] Ibid., Chapter 18, Section "Free will," p 237

[99] Ibid , Section "Consciousness," p. 238

[100] Ibid , Chapter 7 "The origins of language," Section "Why do we talk so much?", p 84

[101] Ibid., p 86

[102] Ibid , Chapter 8, p 93

[103] Ibid., Section "Language spreads memes," p 107

[104] Ibid , p 99; Chapter 9, Section "Memetic drive and Dennett's tower," p 119; Chapter 13 "The altruism trick," Section "Memeplexes and the altruism trick," p 171

[105] Dawkins, *The Selfish Gene*, Chapter 3 "Immortal coils," p 25

[106] Origen himself may have used this word when writing on the epistle to the Hebrews though the evidence is not clear.

Chapter 6

What is a Soul?

> Receiving the end of your faith, *even* the
> salvation of *your* souls.
>
> I Peter 1:9 (KJV)
>
> As the outcome of your faith you obtain
> the salvation of your souls.
>
> I Peter 1:9 (RSV)
>
> obtaining as the outcome out come of
> your faith the salvation of your souls.
>
> I Peter 1:9 (ASV)
>
> for you are receiving the goal of your faith,
> the salvation of your souls.
>
> I Peter 1:9 (NIV)

Writing to God's elect, Peter concludes that the outcome of that redemption won for the elect by Christ is the salvation of their souls. Plainly saving souls is of central importance in God's plan of redemption, but just what is being saved? What is a soul? In this essay we will look at a variety of representative ways that question has been answered, both in Western and in Non-Western traditions. We will begin with a linguistic analysis of the Hebraic and Greek terms, then discuss how attempts by Western philosophers and theologians to systematize the various nuances embraced in those terms modified the meaning of the concept. We will then examine the significance other traditions invested in the idea. Next we will look at contemporary secular accounts of the soul, then we will draw our conclusions.

Section I: Semantic analysis

Drawing its meaning from both Indo-European and Afro-Asiatic languages, the word "soul" has a long and heterogeneous history. Derived from the Old English *sawl*, soul shares a common origin with the word "sea," the supposed habitation of souls in Celtic mythology,[1] but its roots are thousands of years deeper and its ultimate etymology is uncertain. As Indo-European languages, English and Greek are assumed to have a common origin in a hypothetical proto-Indo-European people. Archeologists have yet to uncover such a culture though the Kurgan peoples from the steppe zone north of the Black Sea and beyond the Volga who invaded the Balkans and adjacent regions during the middle of the fifth millennium BC are sometimes proposed as candidates.[2] The Linearbandkeramik or Linear Pottery farmers who may have been among those displaced when the Mediterranean broke through the Bosporus straight and created the Black Sea in 5600 BC are another possibility.[3] However, etymological constructions based on such hypothetical scenarios are highly imaginative. Data from preliterate extinct societies is thin to non-existent, and even among the highly literate Greeks traditions were recorded fairly late and little of it has survived, making it difficult to trace in any detail the development of the idea of soul. From what can be determined, however, it would seem that the Greeks, even into the classic period, were interested, like so many ancient peoples, not primarily in the soul's ultimate destiny but in issues involving this present life. Enough has survived to suggest that in the Archaic age (800 – 500 BC) the Greeks conceived of the soul as a multiple entity consisting of a free-soul or *psuche* representing the individual personality, and one or more body-souls (*thumos, menos*) which motivated specific activities. Then toward the end of the Archaic age *psuche* and *thumos* began to be merge to express the idea of what we would recognize as a centered consciousness.[4]

The Greek word for soul in the I Peter passage is *psuchon*. Derived from *psucho* which means to breathe voluntarily and gently, *psuchon* denotes a sentient principle believed to energize animal life.[5] It is distinct from *pneuma* which in humans refers to the rational principle and is translated as spirit. Angels, demons, and God are also *pneuma*. *Psuche* is distinct as well from *zoe* which refers to mere vitality and can be applied to both animals and plants. Though Hebrew is part of the Afro-Asiatic family of languages, these Greek words have their Hebrew correspondents. The Hebrew word *nephesh* which means either a breathing creature or animal vitality corresponds to *psuche*.[6] Hence in the Septuagint *psuche* is used to translate *nephesh*. *Ruwach*, an onomatopoeic word which can refer to mind, spirit or wind, corresponds to *pneuma*, and is often used to designate powers or actions outside the body, while *chay*, meaning life, corresponds to *zoe*.[7] In Genesis 2:7 when God shapes and breathes life into man, man becomes a living soul (KJV) or living being (RSV, ASV, NIV), that is a *nephesh chay*. It is of the same phrase applied to the beasts of the field in Genesis 1:24.[8] Humanity's unique spiritual component is found not in God's breathing the breath of life into the nostrils of *adam* (Genesis 2:7) but in God's decision to make *adam* "in our own image" (Genesis 1:26).[9] The Hebrews were not given to analytical ontological speculation and tended to view human beings holistically. A person does not have *nephesh* or *ruwach*, but is *nephesh* or *ruwach*, and it is generally agreed, among evangelicals at least, that Paul's anthropology reflects an Hebraic holism rather than Hellenistic dichotomies.

Section II: Western Systematization

However, the three Greek words can also suggest three degrees of soul, a concept Aristotle, who was given to analytical ontological speculation, developed in *De Anima* (On the Soul).[10] Aristotle argued that there were three degrees of soul, degrees that can be described using the three words *zoe*, *psucho*, and *pneuma*. Beginning with the proposition that the soul is in some sense the principle of animal life,[11] Aristotle notes that most people agree the soul is characterized by three marks: Movement, Sensation, and Incorporeality,[12] but that it is itself unmoved.[13] It is the source of movement and sensation and is characterized by them.[14] Though insisting that soul and body must be inseparable,[15] Aristotle distinguishes soul from body,[16] defining soul as "substance in the sense which corresponds to the definitive formula of a thing's essence." It is, he says, " 'the essential whatness' of a body."[17] Soul, according to Aristotle, is that by which "we live, perceive, and think."[18] It is actuality while the body is potentiality.[19] Indeed, soul "is the actuality of a certain kind of body. … [S]oul is an actuality or formulable essence of something that possess a potentiality of being besouled."[20] It is "the cause of source of the living body."[21] It is, he says, "analogous to the hand; for as the hand is a tool of tools, so the mind is the form of forms and sense the form of sensible things."[22] Aristotle then argues that the soul has four forms expressed in powers: the power of touch,[23] the power of appetite, the power of locomotion, and the power of thinking.[24] He then distinguishes between the souls of plants, animals, and men, arguing that all share the nutritive soul which is the most primitive and widely distributed power of soul,[25] while animals also have the power of sensation, locomotion, and imagination, and humans have an additional power to think or calculate.[26]

Aristotle was the first to demarcate three degrees of *psucho*, and his analysis has been tremendously influential in subsequent discussions about the soul, including Christian discussions. For example, Augustine in his *City of God* when critiquing Marcus Varro's belief that the Earth is a deity mentions that Varro distinguishes three degrees of the World Soul: that degree which instills life, that degree which provokes sentience, and the highest degree which is the mind. This last, according to Varro, is God. In human beings he calls it the *genius*.[27] Critiquing Varro's position, Augustine objects to the unnecessary multiplication of deities, asserting that the numerous titles Varro uses number not deities but demons.[28] Instead Augustine, basing his thesis on scriptural references to soul and spirit, argues in *A Treatise on the Soul and Its Origin* (419) that human beings have only "two somethings, soul and spirit," that these two terms can be used interchangeably, and that they refer to the same substance.[29] The soul, he says, is made by God, but its mutability testifies to its being distinct from God.[30] To claim it is a part of God is blasphemous.[31] While the soul derives its life from God, the body derives its life from the soul.[32] Indeed, Augustine says later, "The entire nature of man is certainly spirit, soul and body; therefore who would alienate the body from man's nature is unwise."[33] His argument is plainly intended to defend against doctrines that would denigrate the physical world and is not intended to establish any sharp distinction between spirit and soul. Indeed, Augustine argues that the close identification between soul and body suggests that the soul has gender.[34] Plainly Augustine is far more interested in differentiating between created souls and God, and in defending the goodness of the body as part of God's good creation, than he is in distinguishing between aspects of the soul. And he seems predisposed, perhaps because of the influence of Hebraic anthropology, to view persons in holistic rather than pluralistic terms. Nevertheless, the three aspects *zoe* (bodily vitality), *psucho* (soul), and *pneuma* (spirit) are still discernible, and it is mind (*pneuma*) that differentiates us from the beasts.[35]

Such distinctions were preserved well into the Middle Ages in Christian, Muslim, and, particularly via Moses Maimonides, in Jewish thought. For example, the Scholastics who dominated European metaphysics from the eleventh to the fourteenth centuries differentiated between three types of soul or three aspects of a soul: the vegetative soul which imparted the property of life (analogous to the *zoe*), the sensitive soul associated with animal awareness and shared by humans and other animals (analogous to the *psucho*), and the rational soul (analogous the *pneuma*) which was the seat of critical reflection and was the earmark of human beings. They argued that only the rational soul was immortal, a doctrine they borrowed from Aristotle's belief that the mind alone had the power to exist independently. While Scholasticism was founded on a basic cultural unity that came to dominate Europe and can be traced to the Carolingian empire, it evidenced considerable variety, making sweeping generalizations about the movement problematic. Therefore I shall use as my example Thomas Aquinas not only because he is the best known and most influential of the Scholastics (and probably the most relevant today) but also because his debt to Augustine in this case is explicit and considerable.

Augustine's view on the comparative simplicity of the soul impressed Thomas Aquinas who began his own discussion of the soul by citing Augustine's defense of that simplicity.[36] The soul, Aquinas tells us, is the first principle of life, and life reveals itself in two activities: knowledge and movement. Since not all bodies are alive, we know that no body can be the first principle of life.[37] He defines the human soul as the principle of intellectual operation which is both incorporeal and subsistent. The body provides the soul with sense impressions which the soul interprets.[38] Appealing to Augustine again, Aquinas argues that a human being cannot be reduced to soul and body alone but is both soul and body.[39] Thus Aquinas argues that humans are not essentially souls inhabiting bodies. Nor, he says, does soul refer to a general form that belongs to the species. Human beings are instead a complex of soul and body expressed as individuals.[40] The intellectual principle that is the distinctly human soul, though it relies on a corruptible body, is itself incorruptible. Human souls are distinct from the souls of brutes in this sense: while the souls of animals are generated by some power of the body, the human soul is produced directly by God.[41] This intellectual principle is both the form of the human body and the agency by which we

understand the form of the human body.[42]   Each intellect is individual –
indeed it is impossible that it should be otherwise – and it has primacy
among all other things that pertain to a person.[43]   Furthermore, Aquinas
argues that it is impossible for several essentially different souls to be in a
body, hence the nutritive soul (*zoe*), the sensitive soul (*psucho*), and the
intellectual soul (*pneuma*) are numerically one and the same soul.[44]   In
fact, he argues, the intellectual soul contains the nutritive and sensitive
souls.[45]

The monistic view (defended by Augustine and later Aquinas)
that the soul is the form of the body is, in the opinion of many, a fair
summation of the Christian position.   Certainly through Augustine it had
a profound influence on the Reformers.   Calvin, for example, though he
explicitly rejected Aristotle's assertion that the soul is inseparable from
the body[46] was willing, like Augustine, to use soul and spirit
interchangeably.[47]   Soul is, he said, the essence of a person, separable
from the body, immortal but created[48] out of nothing.[49]   It is the proper
seat of God's image in human beings.[50]   Soul, Calvin maintained, is an
incorporeal substance that, though set in the body in which it dwells as
though in a house, is not limited to the body.[51]   The soul has a variety of
powers,[52] but its two most basic powers are its power to understand and
its power to will.[53]   This definition by Calvin seems to be the one
generally accepted today.   Compare it to three dictionary definitions
selected at random.

According to *Webster's Collegiate Dictionary* (Fifth Edition,
1944) the soul is "an entity conceived as the essence, substance,
animating principle, or actuating cause of life, or of the individual life
manifested in thinking, willing, and knowing.   In many religions it is
regarded as immortal and separable from the body at death...8. A
disembodied spirit." [partial definition]

The Random House College Dictionary Revised Edition (1984)
has a somewhat different definition.   There soul is "1. The principle of
life, feeling, and action in man, regarded as distinct from the physical
body; the spiritual part of man as distinct from the physical part. 2. The
spiritual part of man regarded in its moral aspect, or as capable of
surviving death and subject to happiness or misery in a life to come. 3. A
disembodied spirit of a deceased person." [partial definition]

According to *The American Heritage College Dictionary* (Third
Edition, 1993) soul is "1. The animating and vital principle in human
beings, credited with the faculties of thought, action, and emotion and

often conceived as an immaterial entity. 2. The spiritual nature of human beings, regarded as immortal, separable from the body at death, and susceptible to happiness or misery in a future state. 3. The disembodied spirit of a dead human being, a shade." [partial definition]

Clearly there are differences in the definition given by Calvin and those given by the dictionaries. The concept of soul as substance that one finds in Calvin and in 1944 dictionary has been superseded in the primary definition forty years. later by the concept of soul as immaterial principle while the idea of the soul as something essential to human beings has been lost. The 1984 and 1993 dictionaries, following ancient tradition, use soul and spirit as synonyms while in the 1944 dictionary that point, while there, is not emphasized. This lack of emphasis is especially striking since the definition given for spirit in the 1944 dictionary is quite similar to the one given for soul. But Calvin and all three dictionaries associate soul with volition and awareness, conceived it as distinct from and separable from the body, and assume an individuality to soul that suggests identifiable personality. Finally in all cases soul is understood to have significant religious overtones.

Aristotle, applying reason to the assumptions of his day and structuring that data within the philosophical system he developed, attempted to describe and classify what was meant by soul. His conclusions were both precise and complex. Since then there has clearly been some significant reductionism at work. Though Augustine and Aquinas owe much to Aristotle, they are far more comfortable with the term's ambiguities than was Aristotle, noticeably less precise, and much less willing to attach the kind of importance to shades of meaning that Aristotle saw as significant. Both use soul and spirit as synonyms though they are willing to concede a technical distinction between the words. Calvin, though he has read *De Anima*, owes even less to Aristotle than do Augustine and Aquinas. And today we are likely to find Aristotle's approach even less compelling than Calvin did.

It is striking that both Augustine and Calvin in their discussions of soul are less interested in defining the word than they are in applying certain theological principles to it. In this they differ from Aquinas who does discuss the nature of the soul at some length. Augustine's concerns, as we noted, have more to do with defending the Christian doctrine of creation than they do with clarifying what he means by soul itself. Calvin in his *Institutes* has much to say about the soul but most of his discussion is couched in the terms of forensic salvation. He is more concerned with the soul's care and redemption than he is with its nature.

Before we begin the next part of our discussion, let us pause and formulate our conclusions to this point. Our symbols for soul are derived from natural phenomena like wind, shadows, and sea.[54] Such tropes were an attempt to focus on soul understood as a metaphysical vital principle that existed within living things, that in animals betrayed its presence by activities (particularly breathing), and in humans and sometimes in animals was believed to continue on after death and had significant religious implications. As a continuing vital principle, soul is closely associated with consciousness, especially a concept of consciousness as something that endures after death. Though initially concepts of the afterlife seem less significant, in time pagans like Plato and Aristotle, then Jews, and finally Christians began to associate the soul's survival after death with the idea of a penultimate or a final judgment. Hence, like most metaphysical terms, soul is what Paul Helm has called theory-laden.[55] The metaphors by which we understand soul work insofar as they express what is explicit or implied in whatever world view gave rise to them. For example, if one believes that the universe is fundamentally pluralistic, one's symbols for soul will reflect that pluralism. If one believes that the universe is fundamentally monistic, one's symbols for soul will reflect that monism. Furthermore the term itself is not static but evolves as world views change, and even borrows its meaning from different world views, sometimes mixing distinct traditions. While such eclecticism enriches some terms, it compromise the clarity of others. In the case of "soul" clarity seems to suffer.

Hence some Christian theologians do not like the word soul. Charles W. Carter, for example, believes that "person" or "individual" is a more satisfactory designation in English than is soul since person or individual is a more specific indicator of a self-conscious rational human. He prefers *ego* (or more precisely *ego-psyche*) to *psyche* itself.[56] And many who study non-Christian faiths also find the term soul problematic. Because it is so conditioned by a culture's larger metaphysical world view, and because many cultures do not systematize in the same critical way Western cultures do, it is quite possible that our very "Aristotelian" attempts to criticize and classify other concepts of soul result in our misunderstanding them. However else contemporary ethnographers evaluated nineteenth century efforts by E.B Tylor (*Primitive Culture*, 1871) or early twentieth century efforts by James Frazer (*The Golden Bough*, 1911 – 1915) to organize concepts about the soul, none would affirm the evolutionary paradigm those pioneers used to structure their work. Nevertheless the twelve volumes of *The Golden*

Bough remain a treasure trove of specific information about what so-called primitive societies thought.

Section III: Non-Western Concepts of the Soul

In *The Golden Bough* James Frazer[57] acknowledges this theory laden aspect of the soul and notes:

> As the savage commonly explains the process of inanimate nature by supposing that they are produced by living beings working in or behind the phenomena, so he explains the phenomena of life itself If an animal lives and moves, it can only be, he thinks, because there is a little animal inside which moves it· if a man lives and moves, it can only be because he has a little man or animal inside who moves him The animal inside the animal, the man inside the man, is the soul.[58]

But a soul does not necessarily exist only within one. In some cultures one's shadow or reflection is regarded as one's soul.[59] Nor is the belief in the unity of one's soul necessary or universal. Frazer writes:

> The divisibility of life, or, to put it otherwise, the plurality of souls, is an idea suggested by many familiar facts, and has commended itself to philosophers like Plato, as well as to savages. It is only when the notion of a soul, from being a quasi-scientific hypothesis, becomes a theological dogma that its unity and indivisibility are insisted upon as essential. The savage, unshackled by dogma, is free to explain the facts of life by the assumption of as many souls as he thinks necessary [60]

And Frazer goes on to describe how in different cultures various phenomena are explained by inferring the existence of several souls in each person.

In fact, much of Frazer's argument is based on his observation that across history and around the world conceptions of the soul, its composition, and its powers are myriad. For example, it is believed in many cultures not only that humans and animals have comparable souls, but that a soul can depart the body under certain circumstances and enter other bodies. As a result ceremonies are sometimes contrived to facilitate the transfer of souls between humans and totem animals so that a member of the Wolf clan, let us say, may believe that after undergoing an initiation ritual the wolf's soul dwells in him and his soul dwells in the wolf.[61] This desire to share or exchange souls with an animal is evidence of the profound religious significance animals have for many peoples. Henri Frankfort notes that animals are conscious entities very different from human beings. As such they express an enduring distinctive reality that remains unchanged despite the birth and death of individual members within a given order. Such predestined living patterns appeared to ancient Egyptians to be a manifestation of the divine. As a result Egyptian gods were portrayed as animals.[62] Eliade, investigating shamanism, has also commented on the religious significance for animals among many peoples. They suggest, he says, the possibility of a spiritual life much richer than the life lived by humans. They are believed to have language and to know the secrets of life and nature. Hence the shaman, in an effort to access such knowledge, seeks friendship with animals imitating their behavior or cries.[63] Clearly such conceits, assuming as they do a high level of rationality among animals, require a view of the soul markedly different from the one described in Scripture or posited by most Hellenistic philosophers.

In the modern West we tend to imagine a union between body and soul so absolute that it can only be severed by death, but, as the above examples illustrate, not all cultural complexes make such an assumption. Frazer relates how some people interpret dreams as instances when a soul leaves the body and actually engages in the actions of the dream.[64] But a soul may not only decamp during sleep, it may also get away during waking hours, perhaps escaping from one's mouth while one is eating or drinking.[65] Sickness or insanity may be interpreted as evidence of such a disaster.[66]

The living dead are of central significance in many cultures and are often the focus of a very complex metaphysic. Frankfort, writing about ancient Egypt, provides us with an example. The ancient Egyptians imagined life as a vital force or *Ka* which persisted after death and which always required sustenance. Hence food for the Egyptians had a spiritual dimension, and *Ka* could refer to both the vital principle of life and, when used in its plural form, to that which sustained life.[67] The *Ba*, on the other hand, though it is sometimes translated as soul, is more accurately rendered as "animation" or "manifestation" and refers not to a part of the living person but to the whole person when he or she appears after death.[68]

While few cultures become embodiments of the living dead in the way ancient Egyptian culture did, many do ascribe a high level of importance to "ancestors." Traditional African societies believe that the ancestors after death continue to be interested in and engaged in the affairs of the tribe and can be consulted, generally via spiritual possession. Indeed, such consultations are probably the single most important reason for invoking a possessed state. In Chinese culture even today honors the ancestors with gifts of food and money, and one finds similar beliefs in many other parts of Asia. We will look at a specific example to illustrate one form assumed by such beliefs. In 1968 Robert Gardner and Karl G. Heider published an account of how the Dani in the Grand Valley of Baliem in the Central Highlands of western New Guinea experienced ghosts as an immediate, continual, and essential though sometimes bothersome reality. The Dani believe that all creatures except insects and reptiles possess *etai-eken* ("seeds of singing"). These "seeds of singing," roughly analogous to our concept of soul or personality, and are the most significant elements in human beings. It is interesting to not that they are intimately connected with communication: singing. They first appear near a child's spinal column about six months after birth where they remain until the child begins to speak at which point they move toward the solar plexus where they will take up permanent residence.[69] At death the *etai-eken* are released by shooting an arrow through a small bundle of grass held above the body before it is cremated.[70] In this way an *etai-eken* becomes a ghost. The Dani believe their world is controlled in part by ghosts who afflict them with sickness, bad weather, and spiritual malaise. Thus their religion is concerned primarily with controlling these ghosts.[71] Protecting themselves by magic ritual, the Dani seek to confine ghosts to places called *mokat ai*, usually located about a half mile from the village. It is important for the Dani to do this since ghosts, refined by death, are imagined as more demanding, more meddlesome, more inquisitive, more vindictive, and hungrier than they were prior to death.[72]

One of the most striking things about such accounts is the intimacy they reveal between the living and the dead. In these traditions the ancestors are experienced frequently and directly, so much so that they can become a problem. Clearly those who have these sorts of beliefs consider them to be empirically based. They know from hard experience that the living dead are real. Of course one might argue that they known nothing of the sort, that their "hard experiences" are highly interpreted judgments based upon a metaphysic which in turn validates itself via these judgments. But the objection misses the point, in part because it could be mounted against almost any empirical datum. Of course world views are interpretive and are held by those who, for whatever reason, find them credible. Even beasts seem to have the power of imagination.

Section IV: Contemporary secular accounts

However, from a broader perspective the point about the interpreted nature of empiricism is of significance. Today disciplines like neurobiology and evolutionary psychology are in the process of jettisoning the entire ancient interpretive apparatus we have been discussing in favor of a radically new model of soul, and they are making some powerful empirical arguments to justify its creative demolition.

It could once be claimed that materialists denied the soul exists. This is no longer strictly true. For a host of reasons scientific materialists have been forced to postulate a soul, but they have reinterpreted soul in some very important ways in order to solve some very specific problems. We will look at two such problems: the apparent lack of a center or Cartesian theater in the brain and the need to posit a universal human nature. The first relates to neurobiology, the second to evolutionary psychology.

Since the 1970s studies in neurobiology, particularly of the brain's visual system, have completely undermined the notion that there is a Cartesian theater in the brain which interprets received sensory content. Writing in the September 1992 issue of *Scientific American*, Semir Zeki, professor of neurobiology at University College, London, describes four systems which operating together produce our experience of unified vision. There is a system for motion, one for color, and two for form. One of these systems for envisioning form is interlinked with the system for seeing color, the other is independent.[73] Dr. Zeki also points out that there is no single master area where all of these processes interconnect, that instead there is a vast complex of anatomic links which brings the functioning systems together either directly or via other systems.[74] This suggests, according to Francis Crick and Christof Koch, that consciousness is a process[75] that is distributed over the neocortex.[76] If this model of consciousness is correct, its implications of our understanding of the human soul are revolutionary. Philosophers like John R. Searle, David J. Chalmers, and Daniel C. Dennett have found this scientific model very intriguing. For the sake of brevity, we will consider Daniel Dennett as representative of the group. However, the ideas of these men differ in such marked ways that they disagree, often emphatically and even unpleasantly, with one another.[77]

Daniel Dennett's *Consciousness Explained* is the culmination of a lifetime spent reflecting on the puzzle of what it means to be aware.

His rather startling conclusion is that qualitative, private, subjective experiences or "qualia" do not in fact exist. Instead our inner mental state is the result of a mistake in judgment as outer stimulation triggers an inner reaction.[78] In an analysis obviously influenced by behaviorism, Dennett argues that our ability to discriminate among stimuli is based on various information states that exist simultaneously and, in their mutual interaction, create what we perceive as consciousness. One experience Dennett uses to illustrate what he means is our experience of a unified reality. Experiments have shown that consciousness is not unified. It is instead a patchy affair whose unity appears as the brain fills in the blanks created by the incomplete nature of the stimuli we receive. Consciousness is a whole stitched together from many parts, and its very wholeness is part of its illusion.[79] This wholeness is what we experience as a soul and might even justify the assertion that we have a soul, but that soul is not what Gilbert Ryle would dismiss as "the ghost in the machine." It is instead the accidental emergent creation of the complex interaction of myriad subprocesses, a swarming insectile thing which Dennett compares to the organization of a termite colony. In fact, in a letter to me, Dennett quoted approvingly an Italian journalist's description of his position: "Yes, we have a soul. But it's made of lots of tiny robots."[80] Dennett claims we are descendants of robots,[81] and as such are little more than robots ourselves.[82]

To fully appreciate Dennett's claim that Darwinism reduces us to the level of robots, we should remember that evolution itself has no particular implications for the existence of soul. For example, Alfred Russel Wallace, who is recognized along with Darwin as the co-originator of current evolutionary thought, was a convinced spiritualist. It is rather Darwinian evolution with its materialist implications that presents the real challenge. And if that challenge is apparent when Darwinian thinking is applied to the realm of neurobiology as Dennett has done, it is equally apparent when applied to the field of psychology. Here scholars like Steven Pinker are breaking new ground and drawing some disturbing conclusions.

Steven Pinker refers to the soul as the "traditional explanation of intelligence" and, parodying Ryle, calls it "the spook in the machine."[83] Theories of the soul, Pinker writes, confront the theorizers with two problems: how does this spook, "an ethereal nothing," interact with "solid matter," and what are those who defend the concept of a soul to make of "the overwhelming evidence that the mind is the activity of the brain"?[84] He associates soul with part of that "technique for success" called religion. Religion, he informs us, "is a desperate measure that people resort to when the stakes are high and they have exhausted the usual techniques for the causation of success."[85] Religious beliefs, which are notable for their lack of imagination,[86] are not worth knowing for they merely pile enigmas upon enigmas.[87] In this regard a spirit or soul is simply a cognitive module subject to most natural laws but exempted for others.[88] Such entities are nothing more than "piecemeal revisions of ordinary things."[89] In fact, Pinker opts for a Kantian solution to both religion and philosophy: because the mind is a product of natural selection, it is best at solving practical problems rather than more transcendental ones.[90] The mental equipment necessary to resolve such questions simply failed to evolve.[91]

Although Pinker does not give us an example of such "piecemeal revisions," Jan Bremmer, quoting the Swedish anthropologist A. Hultkrantz, offers one. Noting the early connection between breath and soul, Hultkrantz observers that both are simultaneously material and immaterial, connected to the body but freed from it. He goes on to suggest that the idea expressed in this trope can be imposed over the memory-image of a dead person, thus producing a supernatural reality.[92]

Pinker's ridicule of traditional ideas of the soul is rooted in his contempt for religion, but his philosophical stance is firmly grounded in his rejection of essentialism. He points our that "the driving intuition behind natural kinds is a hidden essence,"[93] that Darwinism is anti-essentialist, and that "In the sciences, essentialism is tantamount to creationism."[94] Yet essentialism, as he points out, seems to be an inborn human attribute.[95] We are, he says, born with "an intuitive physics relevant to our middle-sized world," a physics that accepts matter as enduring and motion as regular.[96] This is of course because the human mind evolved not as an instrument for metaphysical contemplation, but as a tool for solving practical survival problems in an environment where there was greater benefit in the ability to generalize risk than to be precise about it. However, it also evolved in tandem with the lifestyle human ancestors pursued. Though all creatures are related, they are related indirectly in a great bush rather than a great chain, and each species maintains its distinct habits. This means that efforts to rank the intellect of animals is problematic because such efforts assume a general standard when there is no such standard.[97] Just because we evolved from apes, he says, does not mean we have the minds of apes.[98] Paul MacLean's theory of a Triune brain, that is a three-layered brain reflecting our evolution from reptile to primitive mammal to modern mammal, is incorrect. The human cerebral cortex works in tandem with the limbic system rather than riding piggy-back on it.[99]

Although Pinker has been influenced by Dennett and peppers his work with references to the philosopher, he is not a behaviorist. Indeed, he specifically states that behaviorists are wrong.[100] Pinker argues that we do not need "spirits or occult forces to explain intelligence," but neither do we need to "claim that human beings are bundles of conditioned associations."[101] Instead Pinker seeks to use a computational model of the mind to unravel the mysteries of consciousness by wedding it to the theory of the natural selection of replicators,[102] and it is that model of reality that eliminates the need to appeal to a soul. Pinker believes that information is the real juice of the psyche and that emotions are adaptations engineered by genes to work in harmony with the intellect.[103] Hence the major human emotions (anger and fear [this last he argues is a combination of several emotions][104] are his examples) have evolved from precursors like fighting and fleeing.[105] However, he argues that consciousness, which he defines as "being alive and awake and aware,"[106] is essential to moral reasoning.[107] All of which means that Pinker does accept the reality of human universals. The ability to recognize pictures as depictions,[108] the ability to make and recognize facial expressions,[109] and the desire to avoid incest,[110] are among his examples of such universals. Indeed, basing his arguments on the clear results of studies conducted on "thousands of people in many countries," Pinker concludes that human behavior is firmly rooted in genetics and that about fifty percent of the variations in that behavior have genetic causes.[111] There is in Pinker's opinion a recognizable human mind expressing a combination of intellect and emotion, but it is a creation of genes rather than a creation of God. And of course it is this mind he has identified with earlier concepts of the soul. Thus, Pinker implicitly leaves room for a soul but redefines it in some very radical ways.

<u>Section V: Conclusion</u>

To this point we have investigated different ideas as to what constitutes a soul. What can we conclude from this investigation?

First, it seems significant that universally, and for as far back as we can trace, soul and consciousness have been closely associated, so much so that consciousness might be described as the central manifestation or function of soul. It is also of interest that from the beginning consciousness has been ascribed to animals as well as humans, to the degree that animals (or some animals) were believed to possess souls that were, if not divine or semi-divine, then on a par with human souls. Indeed, the degrading of animal souls is a late development, and one that seems suspiciously tied to the kind of rationalism that would eventually lead philosophers like Dennett to the bizarre conclusion that human consciousness is an illusion generated by our robot ancestors as they evolved ever more complex mental machinery. Such a conclusion, counter-intuitive and method-bound as it is, might be grounds for doubting the method that produced it. It seems fair to suggest that a rationalistic approach to understanding the soul, particularly when that approach is based on a mechanistic agenda emphasizing secondary causality, might be wrong-headed. If we are willing to assume with Kant and Pinker that there are questions with which we are ill-suited to grapple, then it is hard to see why a judgment that questions an approach to a problem by pointing out that the conclusions generated by that approach are absurd should not be taken seriously. Rather than analyzing soul too closely, perhaps we should be content to allow some ambiguity in our conception of it, and to admit that attempts to explain soul as a materialistic interplay of cause and effect are doomed to failure.

In this regard we have seen that the definition of soul is fluid, so fluid in fact that it can borrow its meaning from a wide variety of sources and still be used with some degree of intelligibility. We have argued in this regard that the nature of soul as conceived in any given society reflects that society's basic assumptions about the nature of the world. One of the ways we described such assumptions was to call them theory-bound. This observation is unsurprising and may be made of many metaphysical entities.

We have seen that soul can be conceived as unitary or plural, and we have suggested that soul as plural may have historical precedent to soul as unitary. Though I would not want to go so far as Jaynes or even Bremmer and argue that centered consciousness is a late social creation, it does seem arguable from such evidence as we have that soul eventually became a synonym for our experience of centered consciousness. However, given what we know from the Hebraic tradition and the thin evidence from other traditions, I suspect theories as to why this happened (if it did) express little more than our own social presuppositions. It is certainly significant in this regard that despite their various conceptions of the soul, all peoples we know of seem to have a firm awareness of their own centers of being. Just because people do not have a single word for a thing does not mean they have no conception of that thing.

We also noted that old ideas about the soul's plurality survived albeit in a different form in our own tradition for many centuries despite that tradition's basic agreement that the soul was one thing and that individuals were a complex of two things: a soul and a body. In fact the idea of the soul as unitary seems to have become dominant through a process of reductionism. The questions that gave credence to the idea that a soul was plural eventually ceased to be asked, and the unitary nature of soul implicit in the Christian faith, an idea that Christians had inherited from the Jews, was assumed by default. It is interesting in this regard to remember that the Hebrews, who viewed humans as holistic beings, were not given to analytical ontological speculation. Perhaps our own analytical approach to metaphysical questions is as wrongheaded as philosophers like Kant or psychologists like Pinker have suggested.

Concerning the question of reductionism as applied to the soul, it is interesting to note that materialists are monists of a sort. They believe that all is reducible to some kind of stuff. Hence it is unsurprising that materialists like Dennett and Pinker are highly critical of dualism and reject the traditional concepts of soul expressed by dualism. However, a dualism latent in materialism drives them toward affirming some kind of soul. In Dennett's case soul is generated by the body, a position reminiscent of Aquinas' position concerning the souls of animals: they, too, were generated by the body. Ironically Dennett finds himself affirming a position firmly secured in a long dualistic tradition. Pinker fares little better. He wants on the one hand to reject essentialism, yet on the other hand for moral reasons must affirm some universal human distinctives that separate us in quite radical ways from the apes. And after ridiculing the enigmas inherent in theology, Pinker ends by constructing a justification for the enigmas that crop up in his own system, a justification with philosophical roots going back at least to Peter Abelard. Their solutions to the dilemmas confronting them suggest that perhaps dualism is not quite as defunct a tradition as Dennett and Pinker pretend.

Finally, it is fair to ask just what Christian missionaries should teach about the soul when they introduce the gospel into cultures with distinct numinal traditions. In this regard I find the Bible's silence on ontological questions striking. For example, in the Old Testament the unity of God is stressed against the background of deities who had consorts. As Isaiah says: "I am the Lord; and beside me *there is* no saviour." (43:11) "I *am* the first and I *am* the last; and beside me *there is* no God (44:6) "...Is there a God beside me? yea, *there is* no God; I know not *any*." (44:8) "I am the Lord, and *there is* none else, *there is* no God beside me..." (45:5) "...I *am* God, and *there is* none else; I *am* God, and *there is* none like me." (46:9)   Yet such assertions tell us more about God's relationship to other gods (for example, there is no divine consort, no "Mrs. God") than they tell us about God's being. How do we know about God's being? Jesus reveals it to us in the New Testament. Even then the precise nature of God's being is never explicitly defined. Instead, we are left to puzzle it out. That process resulted in the doctrine of the Trinity expressed provisionally in the terminology of Hellenistic philosophy. I suggest that we can infer from this example that God is not in the business of blessing our ontological models, and that the gospel in all its fullness will find comprehending ears in all the world's traditions. It is not our concept of the soul that saves us, it is our faith in the incarnate and risen Lord. This is not to say that we cannot teach some things about the soul: that it is not divine, that it is created, that it needs to be saved, and so forth. But it is to say that we should be less than dogmatic about many of its particulars. God's silence invites us to ponder and participate in his revelation. And indeed it is precisely in that silence where Christianity's incarnational aspects are most apparent.

Endnotes

[1] Celtic myth refers to Otherworld to which one can voyage, or which can be entered through caves or lakes. A place of ambiguous significance, it was also called the Plain of Two Mists, the Land of the Young, the Land of the Living, and the Promised Land, and was believed to lie either in the West beyond the ocean or beneath it

[2] Watkins, Calvert, "Indo-European and the Indo-Europeans," *The American Heritage College Dictionary* (Houghton Mifflin Company, Boston, New York, Third Edition, 1993), p. 1579

[3] Ryan, William, and Pitman, Walter, *Noah's Flood*, Part III "Who Was There and Where Did They Go?", Chapter 18 "Family Trees," p 210

[4] *The Encyclopedia of Religion* (Mircea Eliade, Editor in Chief, Macmillan Publishing Company, New York, 1987), Vol 13, "Soul· Greek and Hellenistic

Concepts" by Jan Bremmer, pp. 434 – 438. This merging has occasioned some speculation that a conscious self actually emerged at the time   Such conjecture can be found in Jan Bremmer's own *The Early Greek Concept of the Soul* (Princeton, 1983) or Julian Jaynes' *The Origin of Consciousness in the Breakdown of the Bicameral Mind* (Houghton Mifflin, 1976)   Sad to say, it has even found its way into the pages of the *Journal of the Evangelical Theological Society* (see Volume 41, Number 1,   March 1998, "After Selfhood. Constructing the Religious Self in a Post-self Age" by Terry C. Muck, pp. 107 – 122).

[5] One might suppose that *psuchon* would be translated as life, that the outcome of our faith is the salvation of our lives, but no one translates *psuchon* as life. All the translations I checked from the New English Bible to the Good News Bible use the word "souls" to translate the passage. Jan Bremmer points out that just because *psyche* once had a connection with breath, it does not follow that such a connection is maintained indefinitely (*The Early Greek Concept of the Soul*, [Princeton University Press, Princeton, New Jersey, 1983],Chapter 1 "The Soul," p 5)

[6] *Nephesh* can also be applied to God. In Leviticus 26:11 or Isaiah 42.1, God, speaking of himself, refers to his own *nephesh*. In the former passage he says, " ..my soul (*nephesh*) shall not abhor you." In the latter he says, " ..my elect *in whom* my soul (*nephesh*) delighteth..."   In such instances soul may be a metaphor for self, or it may be used ontologically.   Whichever is the case, the examples serve to illustrate the term's   ambiguity in Scripture   It was not uncommon among many ancient cultures to address metaphysical questions by employing a variety of approaches rather than appealing to a single coherent theory.   Our insistence on using a single coherent theory to answer our metaphysical questions expresses a cultural bias which developed later

[7] Arabic, also an Afro-Asiatic language, maintains the same distinctions   In pre-Islamic Arabic poetry *nafs* designates blood while *ruh* encompasses the concepts of breath and wind, but in the *Qur'an nafs* refers to the human soul while *ruh* refers to God's spirit. However, Muslims traditionally use *ruh* to refer both to God's spirit and the human spirit. It is worth noting that Islamic philosophers, like Christian ones, borrowed much of their metaphysics of the soul from the Greeks, particularly Aristotle and the neo-Platonists (see *The Encyclopedia of Religion*, "Soul Islamic Concepts" by Michael E Marmura, pp. 460 – 465)

[8] We should note that these Genesis passages eliminate theories, like those expressed by Plato in *Phaedo* or Book X of his *Republic*, of a pre-existing soul. They would also eliminate pantheist philosophies since such philosphies deny the ultimate individually of the soul.   *Adam* becomes a living being after God breathes the breath of life into a form of dust.   This indicates that each individual *adam* has a composite nature, an implication Aquinas develops to defend the unique particularity of each person as we shall see.

[9] I take *adam* to mean both male and female (Genesis 1:27; 5 1 - 2). Given that sexual distinctions are the norm among plants and animals, I do not take that distinction to refer to God's image.

[10] The title of this text is Latin   As knowledge of Greek became a rare accomplishment among Western scholars from the sixth to the middle of the twelfth century, Aristotle was known primarily through Boethuis' Latin translations of his work. From the thirteenth and into the seventeenth centuries a large number of Latin. commentaries on Aristotle were composed.   Richard McKeon notes that if all these Latin texts were collected, their number would exceed the total of everything else that survives (*Introduction to Aristotle*, Random House, New York, 1947, General Introduction, Section 6 "The Influence of Aristotle," p. xxvii). Hence many of Aristotle's works are known by their Latin titles.   It is worth noting that Thomas Aquinas who wrote commentaries on most of the Aristotelian corpus including *De Anima* did so in Latin *Anima* signifies in Latin what *psucho* signifies in Greek   What Aristotle is describing is the *psucho*

[11] Aristotle, *De Anima*, Book I, Chapter 1; Book II, Chapter 2

[12] Ibid , Book I, Chapter 2

[13] Ibid., Chapters 3 through 5

[14] Ibid , Book II, Chapter 2

[15] Ibid. He does note early in his discussion that mind or the power to think seems to be different in kind from other parts of soul and is capable of existence about from other psychic powers.

[16] Ibid , Chapter 1

[17] Ibid.

[18] Ibid

[19] Ibid.

[20] Ibid , Chapter 2

[21] Ibid., Chapter 4

[22] Ibid., Book III, Chapter 8. This is reminiscent of Plato's proposition that a human being is a soul making use of a body. The rational principle of the soul is, according to Plato, the divine element in human beings (*Republic*, Book V,

Chapter 18) and is immortal, an ethical necessity since the soul must reap the consequences of its acts whether good or bad (Book X, Chapter 40)

[23] This power, he asserts, is the primary form of sense (Book II, Chapters 2 and 3, Book III, Chapter 12)

[24] Ibid , Book II, Chapter 3

[25] Ibid.

[26] Ibid , and Book III, Chapter 10

[27] Augustine, *City of God*, Book VII, Chapter 23

[28] Ibid , Chapter 24

[29] Augustine, *On the Soul and Its Origins*, Book II, Chapter 2. In Book IV, Chapter 36 he argues that while the designation *spirit* may be more accurately applied to an aspect of the soul, it is not incorrect to use it as a synonym for soul The question, he says, is one of names rather than things He also says that ignorance about such subtle distinctions puts the believer in no great danger (Book II, Chapter 2).

[30] Ibid , Book I, Chapter 4. Augustine points out forcefully in Book II, Chapter 9, that God's immutability is one of the key dogmas that the doctrine creation from nothing was developed to protect

[31] Ibid , Book I, Chapter 24

[32] *City of God*, Book XIII, Chapter 2

[33] Ibid , *On the Soul and Its Origin*, Book IV, Chapter 3

[34] Ibid., Chapters 32 and 33

[35] Ibid , Book IV, Chapter 35

[36] Aquinas, Thomas, *Summa Theologica*, Book I, Question LXXV, First Article. Aquinas appeals to Augustine's argument as he developed it in *The Trinity*. In fact, throughout his discussion Aquinas appeals repeatedly to Augustine.

[37] Ibid

[38] Ibid , Second Article

[39] Ibid., Fourth Article. Aquinas' reference is *The City of God* Book XIX, Chapter 3, where Augustine commends Varro However, Augustine is concerned that such a position might lend itself to the proposition that the Supreme Good lies in ourselves, therefore he argues in Chapter 4 that it is only when the soul is subordinate to God rather than in control of itself that the body is subordinate to the soul.

[40] Ibid., Question LXXV, Fourth Article

[41] Ibid., Sixth Article This distinction between animal and human souls is particularly significant given the arguments of evolutionists.

[42] Ibid., Question LXXVI, First Article. Aquinas' identification between a form and the agency by which we understand that form reflects Aristotle's debt to Plato Plato, as a means to overcome dualism's epistemological dilemma, identified form and the agency by which we understand form Hence knowledge in Plato's system relies ultimately on intuition. However, Aquinas disagrees with Plato over how the soul comes to know bodies through the intellect. He argues that Plato's opinion that the form of the thing known must of necessity be in the knower in the same way that it is in the known is a mistake. Aquinas denies the necessity of Plato's condition, noting that we perceive variation in the degrees of a quality. This suggests that there is a distinction between the thing itself and the way it is known in the senses (Question LXXXIV, First Article), and, as we saw, Aquinas argued that knowledge comes to the soul via sense impressions mediated by the body. He also defends Augustine against the claim that Augustine's doctrine of knowledge was the same as Plato's by pointing out that Augustine intentionally modified Plato at this point, since he claimed forms, rather than existing in themselves apart from matter, exist as exemplars in the divine mind (Question LXXXIV, Fifth Article), and can also exist in the human soul by their own essence. It is through such exemplars that we understand the information our bodily senses relay to us (Question LXXXIV, First Article) Hence Aquinas argues that, since it is from material things that we acquire our knowledge of immaterial things, our ability to acquire such knowledge is based on our ability to abstract universals from particulars (Question LXXXV, First Article) We understand by composition and division (Question LXXXV, Fifth Article), which is why we can error (Question LXXXV, Sixth Article).

[43] Ibid , Second Article

[44] Ibid , Third Article It would be fascinating to know how Aquinas would have interpreted demon possession, but I am not aware that he wrote on the subject

[45] Ibid., Fourth Article

[46] Calvin, John, *Institutes of the Christian Religion*, Book I, Chapter 1, Section 5 Aristotle based his argument on his belief that the soul as the actuality of the body's potentiality.

[47] Ibid., Chapter 15, Sections 2, 3 and 6

[48] Ibid , Section 2

[49] Ibid , Section 5

[50] Ibid , Section 3.   Calvin dismisses the quarrels of those who distinguish between image and likeness. There is, he says, no difference between the two, and he traces the confusion to the practice of repetition as a literary device among Hebrews.

[51] Ibid., Section 6

[52] Ibid. Calvin lists those he understands as probable but says he is not inclined to argue strongly with those who make a different list

[53] Ibid., Section 7

[54] Birds, too, are often associated with souls, as are insects and small animals like mice   Indeed, many traditions believe the dead manifest as theriomorphs.

[55] *Dictionary of the Christian Church* (J.D. Douglas, general editor, Zondervan Publishing House, Grand Rapids, Michigan, 1974), "Soul" by Haul Helm, p 916

[56] *A Contemporary Wesleyan Theology* Volume 1 (Francis Asbury Press, Grand Rapids, Michigan, 1983), Chapter 6 "Anthropology: Man, the Crown of Divine Creation" by Charles W. Carter, Section 9 "God's Plan for Humanity," sub-section B "Humanity's Relation to the Rest of Creation," p. 210. In this he differs from Bremmer whose analysis depends on a distinction between *psyche* (which he identifies as free soul) and the ego souls under which he groups *thymos* (emotions), *noos* (a thought or a purpose), and *menos* (impulse).

[57] My purpose here is not to defend Frazer. Like most pioneers, he laid the foundations his successors would use to dispute him   But his catalogue of cultural beliefs and practices around the world remains impressive, and will serve to illustrate their variety

[58] Frazer, James, *The Golden Bough* (I Volume, Abridged Edition, The Macmillian Company, New York, 1951), Chapter XVIII "The Perils of the Soul," Section 1 "The Soul as Mannikin," p. 207   This idea of the soul as mannequin is found all over the world, a distribution that suggests it is ancient

Among the ancient Semites *nephesh* was imagined as a diminutive replica of the body (*The Encyclopedia of Religion*, "Soul: Christian Concept" by Geddes MacGregor, p 455).

[59] Ibid , Section 3 "The Soul as a Shadow and a Reflection," p 220

[60] Ibid , Chapter LXVII "The External Soul in Folk-Custom," Section 3 "The External Soul in Animals," p. 800

[61] Ibid , p 802

[62] Frankfort, Henri, *Ancient Egyptian Religion* (Harper & Row, Mew York, San Francisco, London, 1961), Chapter 1 "The Egyptian Gods," Section "Sacred Animals and Otherness," pp. 12 – 14

[63] Eliade, Mircea, *Myths, Dreams, and Mysteries* (Harper & Row, New York, 1975), translated by Philip Mairet, Chapter 3 "Nostalgia for Paradise in the Primitive Traditions," p 63

[64] Frazer, *The Golden Bough*, Chapter XVIII, Section 2 "The Absence and Recall of the Soul," p. 210

[65] Ibid , Chapter XIX "Tabooed Acts," Section 2 "Taboos on Eating and Drinking," p 230

[66] Ibid., Chapter XVIII, Section 2, p 212

[67] Frankfort, *Ancient Egyptian Religion*, Chapter 4 "The Egyptian Hope," Section "The Preoccupation with Death," p. 91. Stevan L Davies in "Soul: Ancient Near Eastern Concepts" (*The Encyclopedia of Religion*. Volume 13) describes it as the power to do (p. 432)

[68] Ibid , Section "The Appearing Dead," pp 96 – 97. The *Ba*, Davies notes, bound together the mummy and the *Ka* ("Soul: Ancient Near Eastern Concepts", p 433). Because some Afrocentric scholars have alleged that precursors of the Christian doctrine of resurrection can be found in the Egyptian *Book of the Dead*, we should point out that Egyptian ideas about the soul's existence in the afterlife are significantly different from the resurrection Christians expect. The *Book of the Dead* is comprised primarily of magic spells intended to protect the soul in the afterlife. The Christian doctrine of resurrection is simply not found there Instead the soul is said to be revived while the corpse remains entombed

[69] Gardner, Robert, and Heider, Karl G., *Gardens of War* (Random House, New York, 1968), Chapter 5 "Ghosts," pp. 87 – 88. Gardner and Heider mention later (p 91) that some Dani believe that only humans have *etai-eken.*

[70] Ibid , p. 95

[71] Ibid , p. 93

[72] Ibid , pp 88 – 89

[73] *Scientific American* (September, 1992, Volume 267, Number 3), "The Visual Image in Mind and Brain" by Semir Zeki, p. 73

[74] *Ibid* p. 75

[75] *Ibid*, "The Problem of Consciousness" by Francis Crick and Christof Koch, p 153

[76] *Ibid*, p. 158

[77] For an example of such disagreement, I call the reader's attention to an exchanged published in *The New York Review of Books* as John R. Searle reproduces it in *The Mystery of Consciousness* (NYRV, Inc., 1997), Appendix to "Conscious Denied· Daniel Dennett's Account," pp. 115 – 131.

[78] Dennett, Daniel, *Consciousness Explained* (Little and Brown, Boston, 1991), Chapter 12 "Qualia Disqualified"

[79] Ibid., Chapter 11 "Dismantling the Witness Protection Program," pp 355 – 366

[80] On page 367 of Chapter 11 in *Consciousness Explained*, Dennett describes souls as "mathematical abstractions rather than nuggets of mysterious stuff They're exquisitely useful fictions." Notice the vast disconnect between reality and our way of thinking about reality that is implied in Dennett's remark Apparently mathematicians, as they attempt to consider questions of magnitude or relationship in a systematic way, use nothing real. Instead their abstractions are exquisitely useful fictions.

[81] Dennett, *Darwin's Dangerous Idea* (Simon & Schuster, New York, 1995), Part II "Darwinian Thinking in Biology," Chapter 8 "Biology is Engineering," section 4 "Original Sin and the Birth of Meaning," p 206. Here Dennett writes, "Well, if Darwin is right, your great-great ... grandmother *was* a robot! A macro, in fact That is the unavoidable conclusion of the previous chapters Not only are you descended from macros, you are composed of them."

[82] John Searle in his section on Dennett in *The Mystery of Consciousness* makes this very plain He writes, "This looks as if [Dennett] is claiming that sufficiently complex zombies would not be zombies ... but.. [h]is claim is that in fact *we are*

zombies.. The claim is not that the sufficiently complex zombie would suddenly come to conscious life... Rather Dennett argues that there is no such thing as conscious life..., there is only complex zombiehood " (pp 106 – 107)

[83] Pinker, Steven, *How the Mind Works* (W W. Norton & Company, New York, London, 1997), Chapter 2 "Thinking Machines," p. 64. Pinker is so eager to express his contempt for traditional religious conceits that he misuses the word "spook," equating it with the intellectual soul. Jan Bremmer points out that a spook is better thought of not as a real personality but as an aspect of the person (his emotions, impulses, desires, etc.) that survives death. He also states that spooks are commonly associated with thoroughly dualistic traditions (*The Early Greek Concept of the Soul*, Chapter 3 "The Soul of the Dead," p 76   Quoting Hultkrantz, Bremmer notes that the "spook-ghost [is] a distorted by-product, a remote echo of the departed individual. ", p. 83). The real personality that survives death is more closely associated with what Bremmer calls the freesoul, and it is this soul which is associated with intelligence (Chapter 2 "The Soul of the Living," p. 51). Pinker's gaff reveals both his contempt for and his ignorance of soul traditions.

[84] Ibid. Notice that to raise such an objection Pinker dematerializes soul altogether while retaining matter's solidity. In an era where advances in physics have resulted in what some have called the dematerialization of matter, and where, according to Einstein, spinning objects might be able to pull the empty space around them in a swirling circle (a hypothesized phenomenon called "frame dragging"), this move seems strange, but besides noting its strangeness, I will not discuss it here.

[85] Ibid., Chapter 8 "The Meaning of Life," p. 556

[86] Ibid., p. 557. That seems like an odd reason to criticize the truth claims of an idea   Surely a more traditional reason for rejecting a conclusion would be the objection that it is too imaginative!

[87] Ibid , p 560

[88] Ibid., p. 556

[89] Ibid , p 557

[90] Ibid , p 525

[91] Ibid., pp. 562 – 563

[92] Bremmer, Jan, *The Early Greek Concept of the Soul*, Chapter 2 "The Soul of the Living," p 23. He uses the word <u>producing</u> rather than <u>expressing</u>

[93] Pinker, *How the Mind Works*, Chapter 5 "Good Ideas," p. 324

[94] Ibid., p. 325

[95] Ibid , pp. 326 – 327

[96] Ibid., p. 321

[97] Ibid , Chapter 3 "Revenge of the Nerds," p. 182

[98] Ibid , Chapter 1 "Standard Equipment," pp. 23, 40. In Chapter 3, he lists some of those differences (pp 186 – 187) and insists "that there is no such thing as an 'ape legacy' that humans are doomed to live by" (Chapter 7 "Family Values," p 465) But lest we go overboard with the implications of all this, Pinker reminds us that "real science" recognizes that "people are apes" (Chapter 5, p 309).

[99] Ibid., Chapter 6 "Hotheads," pp. 370 – 371. MacLean's theory has received a great deal of attention in popular publications (see, for example, Carl Sagan's Pulitzer Prize winning *The Dragons of Eden* [Ballantine Books, New York, 1977])

[100] Ibid , Chapter 5, p. 329

[101] Ibid., Chapter 2, p 92

[102] Ibid , Preface, p. ix

[103] Ibid., Chapter 6, p. 370. He understands intelligence as a capacity naturally selected by evolution to exploit a "cognitive niche " (Chapter 3, p 200)

[104] Ibid , pp 386 – 387

[105] Ibid , p 416

[106] Ibid., Chapter 2, p 134

[107] Ibid , p 148. In Chapter 8, on page 558, Pinker specifically equates consciousness, sentience, and subjective experience, just in case there is any doubt about his meaning. Furthermore, Pinker has strong moral concerns that underlie what he says. When addressing the question whether humans are still evolving, he lists several reasons to believe they are not. Among those reasons is human vice which he sees as proof that human evolution is a thing of the past (Chapter 3, p. 207). And he denies that what comes naturally is always good (Chapter 7, p 492).

[108] Ibid , Chapter 4 "The Mind's Eye," 214

[109] Ibid., Chapter 6, pp. 365 – 366

[110] Ibid., Chapter 7, p. 456

[111] Ibid., p 448

Conclusion

On December 5, 1998, *The New York Times*, in honor of Noam Chomsky's seventieth birthday, ran an article by Margalit Fox in which the linguist discussed a new idea he had been exploring since the early 1990s, an idea he called the Minimalist Program for a universal grammar that would make language acquisition possible. Warming to his subject, Chomsky asked the reporter to imagine that a divinity endowed humans with the power of language, a power that would enable humans to identify specific sounds with specific meanings, and, Prof. Chomsky supposed, would have been given to humans all at once and would be designed to be as simple as possible.[1] While the context of the article makes it clear that Chomsky's appeal to a divine designer is intended not as serious theology but as a means to illustrate the nature of the problem he is trying to solve, it is revealing. Communication of the kind we are discussing goes far beyond cause and effect. It is based on both identity and intuition, and hence is predicated on some intuitive ability to grasp something of the subjective state of the other. It is, as we have argued, interpretive (as evidenced by the fact that it can deceive and be deceived), and is based on stimulus and response. And it seems to express something deeply rooted in the very fabric of reality. Chomsky's willingness to jettison almost half a century of work and to illustrate his new beginning by appealing to divine agency captures our sense of the problem. Communication is not fundamentally an expression of interacting compounds plucked from the periodic table. It is instead evidence of the other reality: the existence of an abstractive, intuitive soul. Like the elements of the periodic table, it is a reality given by God, but unlike those elements, it operates on a different set of laws, and it is cognizant.

However, communication abilities, being in large measure species specific, suggest that soul does share a quality with chemical elements: it comes into or goes out of existence as a particular thing. It does not evolve. It interacts with its environment and in this sense changes, but its changing is an expression of its latent potential. It remains essentially what it is. Even as humans are basically the same,[2] and communicate best with human beings, so other species communicate best among members of their own kind. While some basic ideas may be transmitted across species, even as oxygen and hydrogen might interact despite being fundamentally different, the subtleties that fill in the finer shades of meaning are lost. Species do not perceive the world or react to the world in the same way and hence cannot communicate their distinct realities to one another. They simply lack sufficient common ground. Courtship rituals are one evidence of such differences, territorial markings another. A bird and a human being may see the same automobile, but they do not see the same thing when they see that automobile. Though a cat can see shape and shade, it cannot see art. Though a dog can hear volume and pitch, it cannot hear music. While we may infer from this that the world we perceive is richer world than the world perceived by cats and dogs, we really have no way to judge the truth of that inference. All we can assert for certain is that ours is a human world and therefore different. The qualities that distinguish the human world from the world of a cat or the world of a dog lie beyond our human horizons since, being neither cats or dogs, we cannot perceive as they do. This is evidenced by our inability to communicate meaning to cats and dogs in any but the most basic ways.

And what is true among contemporary species is probably true if applied to those which are extinct. Take Neanderthals for example. Classified as *Homo neanderthalensis* or sometimes *Homo sapiens neanderthalensis*, the species is usually considered to have endured approximately 95,000 years, having arisen roughly 130,000 years ago and having died out about 35,000 years ago,[2] or about five thousand years after the ancestors of modern Europeans are believed to have begun their invasion of that continent. It's range probably extended across Europe and into the Middle East. Short and immensely powerful, its members controlled fire, dug hearths in the floors of caves in which they occasionally lived (these are the classic "cave men"), made tools, and sometimes buried and sometimes ate their dead.   What was their relationship to us, and upon what data can we base our conclusions?

While we are assumed to share the same genus, along with *Homo habilis* and *Homo erectus*, the relationship between Neanderthal and modern humans is uncertain as the variations in classification demonstrate.[3] The data of course is thin and has come to light fairly recently. In 1848 a skull cap was found in Forbes's quarry at the Rock of Gibraltar. In 1864 that fossil was matched with a similar one found in

1856 in the Neanderthal valley in Germany, and both were classified as Neanderthal man.[4] Those were the earliest finds. By the beginning of the 1960s, the fossil remains of only about fifty-five western Neanderthals were known. Many of these are too fragmentary to allow for any detailed description of the individuals they represented. Some had been lost.[5] While Neanderthal data has expanded somewhat in the intervening years, and now comes from something over seventy sites, it remains very thin, and its scarcity enables us to interpret it in a variety of ways as the following questions will illustrate.

Did Neanderthals talk? Voicing the general consensus of the early in the twentieth century anthropologists, H.G. Wells wrote that Neanderthals probably lacked any developed language.[6] The growing consensus today seems to be that they probably did, but without the vocal range that we enjoy. Some scientists have argued that the higher larynxes of the Neanderthals would have made speech difficult if not impossible, but those larynxes may have been an adaptation to the cold as their appearance seems to coincide with a period of intense glaciation when higher larynxes and larger sinuses would have been advantageous for warming cold dry air. Were that the case, speech, if it already existed, may have developed in a way to compensate for the change in the position of the larynx. And the fossil evidence indicates that speech may have existed since the hypoglossal canal which carries the nerves that control the tongue reached its current size about 300,000 years ago.[7] However, the recent discovery of a Neanderthal hyoid bone has led some anthropologists to argue that the Neanderthal larynx was identical to ours.[8]

If they spoke, they had a social life since language is by definition a social instrument, but it may have been a very different social life from the one we enjoy, so they probably expressed ideas very different from our own.[9] What was Neanderthal social life like? It's particulars elude us. It is tempting to imagine that it was not unlike our own, but, given the wide variety of social conventions *Homo sapiens* are known to have practiced, and given that much of that practice developed around some kind of settled community which Neanderthals probably did not have, such a conjecture, even if it did not mislead us, would tell us very little. There is also the possibility that it was quite different from our own. Lewis Binford, basing his conclusions on archeological evidence, argues that Neanderthals were not very good at making plans and to imagine scenarios that would enable them to adjust to their changing world.[10] He also believes that Neanderthal men and women lived apart, ate different food, and that the males saw the females only briefly between foraging trips.[11]   Hence lasting bonds were not formed and there is nothing we would recognize as a traditional family life.[12] Certainly such a model of Neanderthal society is at odds with the model assumed by Morton who also constructs his argument on the archeological evidence.   Remember here that such arguments rely on the absence of evidence (no Neanderthal remains found in the grasslands) or can turn on a single piece of evidence (an object believed to be a flute). It is interesting speculation and wakens us to possibilities, but it should be taken with a large pinch of salt.

Did Neanderthals have music or art? Again the evidence, thin as it is, suggests the answer may be yes, at least as a late development. Morton notes the discovery of what appears to be a flute hewn from a bear bone approximately 43,000 years ago at a Neanderthal site at Divje Babe in Slovenia. He also refers to leopard bones arranged in a way that would suggest that had once been part of a shaman's coat, this found at a Neanderthal site at Hortus, France, and dating to about 50,000 years ago. In 1996 a possible Neanderthal sanctuary deep in a cave was discovered at Bruiniquel, France.   Built approximately 47,000 years ago, this "sanctuary" consisted of a thirteen by sixteen foot rectangular structure inside of which were charred bear bones. Morton also refers to a Neanderthal site in Nahr Ibrahim, Lebanon, in which a deer had apparently been ritually prepared and sprinkled with red ocher (possibly a symbol for blood?) that was chemically distinct from the red ocher found at the cave itself and must have been carried in from elsewhere. Morton sees this as evidence of some ability to plan ahead.[13]   It is certainly evidence of some ability to think abstractly and to symbolize and communicate one's thoughts.

This observation leads quite naturally to the question: did Neanderthals have a concept of the afterlife? If they had religious ritual, which Morton plainly believes they did, then it would be surprising if they had no idea of life after death. And in fact, the discovery of Neanderthal graves suggests that they had such a concept. Perhaps the best known example of such a grave is the one found at Shanider Cave in Iraq where it appears that approximately 50,000 years ago in the early period of the Wurm glaciation[14] and probably between late May and early July (based on the type of pollen found in the grave) a Neanderthal man was buried on a bed of branches and flowers.[15] However, the remains of six individuals, two adults, two teenagers, and two children, dating about 100,000 years ago and found in a cave at Moula-Guercy in the Ardeche region near the Rhone River in southeastern France, also provides evidence that Neanderthals occasionally practiced cannibalism. If the site does preserve a cannibal feast, the reason for the cannibalism cannot be determined, though the way the remains were butchered and scattered around the site suggests something more akin to the slaughtering of game than to ritual.[16] This feast and the evidence compiled by Lerot-Gourham and Morton is separated by some fifty thousand years. That is a time lapse of sufficient duration to cause us to wonder if some kind of spiritual awakening might have occurred during the interim. Yet culture seems to have changed quite slowly in the ancient past. For example, in the Ardeche region, to which we have already referred, some two hundred caves are known in which depictions of mammals, many of them now extinct, are preserved. These depictions are Cro-Magnon work and were done in roughly the same style and the same way over a period from 30,000 to 17,000 years ago.[17] They were, as Robert Hughes, paraphrasing Claude Levi-Strauss pointed out, "good to think with."[18] It is striking not only that such a thought world developed, but that it seems to have been so closely identified with a single region and so conservative.[19] This conservatism has been suggested as well in the possible origins and longevity of the cave bear cult mentioned above. Did Neanderthals believe the same thing for the ninety-five to one hundred thousand years they roamed Europe and western Asia? It seems unlikely, in which case the juxtaposition of earlier Neanderthal cannibalism and later Neanderthal ritual might be significant, but, given the paucity of the evidence and the apparent conservatism of ancient cultures, who can say?

Did *Homo neanderthalensis* interbreed with *Homo sapiens*? Here the evidence is equally inconclusive. In the middle of the twentieth century there was much excitement over the discovery of evidence comprised of a high level of individual variety and mixed tool forms at Mount Carmel caves in Palestine that suggested to some that interbreeding between the two groups may have taken place there.[20] Had such interbreeding occurred, it would mean that *Homo neanderthalensis* was simply a local variant or subspecies of *Homo sapiens* as the classification *Homo sapiens neanderthalensis* suggests, but the fossil evidence for it was slight. Genetics suggested that it had not taken place. Studies of mitochondrial DNA implied that living *Homo sapiens* originated approximately 100,000 years ago, replacing but not breeding with *Homo neanderthalensis*.[21] However, the possibility of interbreeding continues to be proposed as new fossils come to light. A skeleton of what was probably a four-year-old boy excavated near Leiria, Portugal, eighty miles north of Lisbon, in December 1998, and dated to 24,500 years ago, appears to be a hybridization between Neanderthal and more modern humans. With its prominent chin, short limbs and stocky body, the specimen has reawakened speculation that such interbreeding did occur and was not rare.[22]

There you have it: *Homo neanderthalensis* did or did not speak, may or may not have had music and art, probably had a social life though one very different from our own, either buried or ate their dead, and may or may not have been able to interbreed with *Homo sapiens*. If all that seems a bit uncertain, it is only because the scant evidence couple with our own imaginations make it so since *Homo neanderthalensis* must have been some way, we simply do not know what way. Which means that at this point we do not know what kind of relationship *Homo neanderthalensis* and *Homo sapiens* actually shared, though we may assume that at least for a time a relationship existed. It is therefore impossible to assess the significance of that relationship. While I would argue that they had souls, I would also argue that dogs and cats have souls. Beyond that the evidence is far too plastic to allow us to draw many conclusions with any certainty. It follows that that as they are currently known, *Homo neanderthalensis* as a concept while anthropologically useful is theologically irrelevant, or almost so. Could we contrive a meeting with a group of Neanderthals, communication would, I suspect, be most imperfect. Such language as they might have would doubtless be constructed around different realities and used to express different needs. If the stories we read from the clay tablets of Ur seem strange to us, how much stranger might the stories told by Neanderthal shaman to neophytes in the depths of caves sound. And perhaps they told no stories but communicated their impressions by other means.

In this study I have based my thesis on conceptualist philosophy coupled with the insights of neurobiology, but one might make a similar case using quantum theory. The mathematician Peter Zoeller-Greer has written a most interesting essay in which he argues that conditioned reality, being created by observation, is not unique but variable, and that if we want to access the true account of creation (for example), we must listen to God's version in the first chapter of Genesis rather than rely on our own conceits.[23] After all, that account is God's and the theologically significant one while evolution in its various forms is the tale we tell ourselves.

Science, it is often observed, is less about proof than about valid inference. But inference rests in large measure upon belief. Part of the issue here is that while belief cannot be constrained, assent may be. The experiment which can predict compels assent but cares nothing for belief since belief is a question of interpretation. After all, quantified prediction can hardly be denied. But interpretation is fundamentally inferential because interpretation rests in large measure on plausibility, and plausibility rests on belief. For example, how plausible are Darwinian descriptions of the emergence of complexity? That will depend on one's initial suppositions.

The emergence of complexity from simplicity has always been one of the central conundrums of Darwinism. Darwin in addressing this problem attempted to explain complexity by confounding it with perfection. For example, using breeds of domestic animals and plants as an analogy for what he believed occurred in nature, Darwin argued that even as breeders worked to improve their stocks, so nature strove unconsciously toward perfection via a process of continuous improvement through competition.[24] Notice that perfection here is understood as embracing ever greater variety or complexity. Indeed, Darwin, who imagined a Malthusian world in which abundant life was inevitable, stated as a principle that "the greatest amount of life can be supported by great diversification of structure."[25] However, from a metaphysical standpoint, perfection is generally associated not with complexity but with simplicity since complexity introduces the possibility improvement while perfection assumes an excellence beyond improvement.[26] Thus theologians assert the simplicity of God as a means of underlining his absolute perfection. The Taoist virgin block would be another example. One might argue that nature via some strange alchemy goes though a stage of complexity on the way from chaos (the Big Bang or some such thing) to simplicity (absolute zero or whatever), but then how does one account for the emergence of complex life from matter that is more simply organized (i.e. more stable)? Darwin, though he would not have formulated the issue in quite this way, was clearly aware of the problem and attempted to account for complexity by appealing to the principle of Natural Selection.[27] In Darwin's view life in competition with life and always producing more life s pawned complexity as a natural consequence. But it is not easy to see why that should be. One might just as well see complexity as "unnatural" precisely because, as an interrelated composite, it is less stable and less likely to have come into existence, especially in any highly organized form. And one might argue that such complexity is evidence of creation. Hence in the sixth chapter of *The Origin of Species* Darwin, as he discussed difficulties he perceived with his theory, wrote: "If it could be demonstrated that any complex organ existed, which could not possibly have been formed by numerous, successive, slight modifications, my theory would absolutely break down."[28]

Critics of Darwin have addressed that challenge in several ways. Some have pointed out that the reality of miracles contradicts the Darwinian worldview which is a primary reason that so many scientists accept as a given that miracles cannot occur. After all, miracles are immediate creative acts of God that are not explicable by an appeal to numerous, successive, slight modifications. If one accepts them, one has no need to appeal to evolution to explain the world. Others have claimed the eye, before which Darwin himself trembled, as a candidate for an organ that could not have developed in an exclusively Darwinian way. Others have argued that life's origins cannot be accounted for in purely naturalistic terms. Behe's concept of irreducible complexity when applied to the chemical processes of life is another effort to respond to Darwin's challenge. To this I add communication phenomena. Such phenomena, because they are based on intuition, stimulus and response, and the ability to interpret the meaning of symbols,[29] extend far beyond the material and secondary causality that informs the scientific process and point to realities closed to that process. Yet communication, rather than being unique, is a common feature in nature. This points to a reality beyond the material, a reality of consciousness, intelligence,[30] soul, for only in that realm can abstract communication take place. Indeed, historically communication has been ascribed as a peculiar function of the soul. Only since the nineteenth century and for largely philosophical reasons has the idea of communication has a function of machines become popular.

To capture something of the nature of that paradigm shift, one should remember that Darwin as he constructed his argument occasionally contrasted his own ideas with the then accepted idea that species had been created by divine fiat. In making his contrasts, Darwin argued that such a thesis raises many questions that his counter proposal resolves nicely. But notice this: the idea that divine creation and science are incompatible is not an idea entertained by Darwin. It is an idea that came into ascendancy only in the twentieth century as a consequence of the perceived necessity of science *qua* science to construe natural phenomena solely in terms of material secondary causality. Descent with modification as an exclusive explanation fits neatly into such an agenda, but it is not necessarily the best or the simplest way to address the mystery of existence. It is instead an approach one chooses if one is committed to a particular philosophical position.

Notice too that this emphasis on material secondary causality invites us to conclude either that prior to the twentieth century no one was doing true science or that the idea of creation is not inimical to scientific theory. Indeed, one might argue that the design implied in the creation model is what makes the orderly investigation of nature possible and is the very thing science ought to explore. It is of interest to note that accounting for apparent order in a universe assumed to be chaotic has become a problem only with the general abandonment of the creation model. Return to that model and the problem largely disappears.

The same is true of the problem of communication. It we assume a dual reality, one of matter and one of soul, both interacting and yet expressing distinct properties, accounting for the fact of communication ceases to be a problem. Of course one might investigate a host of other problems inherent in the phenomenon itself, but the brute fact that organisms exist that can produce and communicate abstract ideas is no longer an issue. It is instead a given. On the other hand, if one limits reality to matter, then consciousness, communication, the capacity to represent ideas symbolically, the existence of reason, and a whole host of other common phenomena become quite inexplicable. Of course the materialist would insist they are properties latent within matter or certain configurations of matter. Yet how would this be tested? Even if machines could be designed to ape such properties, it would prove nothing about the latent properties of matter precisely because the machines would have been *designed* to *imitate*. Design is what the materialist denies. Imitation as an effect of design tells us nothing about a property alleged to be latent in something and to have come into existence without benefit of design. Our ability to build adding machine no more accounts for the properties of arithmetic than our ability to build musical instruments accounts for the phenomenon of music.

Communication is a property of soul in the same way occupation of space is a property of matter.[31] The materialist fails precisely by confounding these two realities and then inappropriately applying the properties of one to the nature of the other. There is nothing "natural" in the materialist view. It is a way of thinking in which one must be trained. What is far more natural is the view that a unique principle or set of principles accounts for the reality we know through experience: the reality of a centered self that is aware and able to communicate its awareness both to itself and to others like itself. Materialism cannot adequately account for such phenomena, nor, I believe, can evolution, even a spiritualized form of evolution. Such abilities are attributes of that which is endowed by God. The aware self able to communicate with other aware selves is qualitatively distinct from insensible selfless matter and did not evolve from it. It was created by fiat from nothing. God's capacity to do that is the capacity to which Berdyaev referred when he talked about creative acts as rooted in nothing and having no predicates beyond God's unconstrained ability to create by calling those things which be not as though they were. That is the reality to which miracles attest, and if one has miracle, one has no need of evolution.

Awareness, symbolism, and communication lie at the foundation of worship, and worship is the highest form of communion with God. It is for that purpose we were made, and it is in worship that we participate in the infinite and reveal our destiny as eternal beings. Hence to a child's question, "Are there such things as ghosts?" we might respond, "Of course there are. The two of us are talking, aren't we?"

Endnotes

[1] *The New York Times*, Saturday, December 5, 1998, Section B, "Arts and Ideas/Cultural Desk," "A Changed Noam Chomsky Simplifies" by Margalit Fox, column 1, page 7

[2] These dates are conservative. Some sources put Neanderthals in a time range of 300,000 to 30,000 years ago. The issue is not so much when they died out. That date is more secure and corresponds with the appearance of *Homo sapiens*. The question instead is how far back did Neanderthals go.

[3] One of the points we have consistently stressed is how our categories of classification structure the way we imagine origins. In this case our decision on how to relate Neanderthal to modern humans will depend on how inclusive or exclusive our definition of species is. *Sapiens* embraces a great deal of physical variety, and by definition those fossil specimens we class as *sapiens* would have their counterparts among living specimens today.

[4] Coon, Carleton S., *The Origin of Races* (Alfred A. Knopf, New York, 1962), Chapter 11 "The Caucasoids," Section "The 'Neanderthals' of Europe," p. 519. My use of this book might raise some eyebrows since many anthropologists have condemned Coon as racist (see, for example, *The Concept of Race* [Crowell-Collier Publishing, New York, 1964], a collection of essays edited by Ashley Montagu and specifically intended to rebut Coon). However, Harry

Jerison in *Evolution of the Brain and Intelligence* (Part IV "Progressive Evolution and the Brain," Chapter 16 "The Primates and Man," pp 400 - 402) praises *The Origin of Races* for its catalogue of Neanderthal fossils and is particularly enthusiastic about the data Coon provides for the Steinheim cranium, discovered in July 1936 in a gravel pit at Steinheim an der Murr in Wurttemberg, twelve miles north of Stuttgart, and the Swanscombe fragments (these sections "The Steinheim Cranium" and "The Swanscombe Cranial Bones" appear on pages 492 - 497 of *The Origin of Races*). It would seem that one can applaud Coon's research without necessarily ascribing to his conclusions. I certainly do not subscribe to Coon's conclusions, but find his compilation of, and interpretation of, Neanderthal data instructive.

[5] Ibid , Section "The Western Neanderthals," p 527. In the preceding section "The Numbers and Distribution of the Neanderthals" Coon details the various fragments and identifies the locations where they were found.

[6] Wells, H. G., *The Outline of History* (Doubleday and Company, Garden City, new York, 1961), Volume I, Book II "The Making of Man", Chapter 7 "The Neanderthal Men, An Extinct Race," section 2, p. 62

[7] As reported on MSNBC in April 1998.

[8] Morton, Glenn R., "Dating Adam," *Perspectives on Science and Christian Faith* (Vol. 51, No 2, June 1999), Section "Language," left hand column, p. 91

[9] Fischman, Joshua, "Hard Evidence," *Discover* (February 1992), pp. 44 - 51

[10] Ibid., pp. 48, 51   One of the evidences Binford sees for his conclusion is the absence of Neanderthal remains in what would have been the vast grasslands of the period   Game would have been plentiful there, so why did Neanderthals fail to exploit it? Binford suggests it is because they were not capable of the long range planning necessary for conducting such a hunt. Lions can do that, but in Binford's opinion Neanderthals could not. However, MSNBC news reported that a study co-authored by Paul B. Pettitt of Oxford University in England and Erik Trinkaus of Washington University in Saint Louis compared the isotopic ratios of nitrogen in the jawbones and skulls of 28,000-year-old Neanderthal remains found in a cave in Croatia. The study indicated that about 90% of the Neanderthal diet consisted of meat. The authors of the study which appeared in the June 2000 Proceedings of the National Academy of Sciences argued that this implies that Neanderthals could organize complex hunts.

[11] Ibid., p. 48

[12] Ibid., p. 50

[13] Morton, "Dating Adam," *Perspectives on Science and Christian Faith* (Vol. 51, No 2, June 1999), Section "Religion," p. 94. Morton hypothesizes that the cult of the cave bear may have originated with Neanderthals, and been passed through them to *Homo sapiens* This is a claim that is decades old and is based on discoveries of sites like the one in Drachenloch (Dragon's Lair) in the Swiss Alps where a rock chest containing the skulls and leg bones of seven cave bears was discovered. The arrangement of the skulls and leg bones evokes in us the sense that some kind of ritualistic intent may have been expressed (Howell, F. Clark, *Early Man* [Time-Life Books, New York, 1965], Chapter 6 "Just Who Was Neanderthal?", pp. 126 - 127; Chapter 7 "The Dawn of Modern Man," p 154), and is one of the reasons why Morton considers Neanderthals and Cro-Magnons varieties of the same species. If so, this cult, which must have been nearly universal at one time, may have endured longer than any other religion. Carlos Ginzburg in his book *Ecstasies* (Hutchinson Radius, 1990), a study of the witches' sabbath, suggests that the hairy hand of the goddess Diana, patroness of the hunt, the night, and the moon, might be a holdover from the Paleolithic when she was a snarling bear.

[14] It is usually agreed that the Wurm began about 70,000 years ago.

[15] Lerot-Gourham, Ariette, "The Flowers Found with Shanidar IV," *Science* (Vol 190, No , 4214, November 7, 1975), pp 562 - 564

[16] Witze, Alexandra, "Find called best evidence yet of Neanderthal cannibalism," *The Dallas Morning News*, Friday, October 1, 1999, p. 24A; Golden, Frederic, "A Repast for Neanderthal," *Time Magazine*, October 11, 1999, p. 75. Robert Kunzig in "The Face of an Ancestral Child," *Discovery* (December 1997) describes a similar find between 1994 and 1996 at Gran Dolina in Atapuerca in northern Spain of six individuals dated at approximately 800,000 years ago. They are the oldest known human remains in Europe and half of the eighty-six bones recovered show evidence of having been butchered. The way the bones were broken and stripped suggests that the butchers were after the marrow, and that along with the early date suggests that ritual was not behind the killings (right hand column, p. 100). F. Clark Howell also refers to a site at Krapina in what was then Yugoslavia where burned and smash Neanderthal bones were found. He suggests a cannibal feast took place here as well and that such feasts may have had ritualistic meaning (*Early Man*, Chapter 6, p. 134). It seems significant that, as thin as Neanderthal evidence is, so many "cannibal sites" have been discovered. This suggests the practice might have been common. Interestingly H. G. Wells in his *Outline of History*, quotes Sir Harry Johnson who wondered if the Neanderthals, powerful, slightly grotesque, and prone to cannibalism, "may be the germ of the ogre of folklore" (Chapter 8 "The Later Paleolithic Age and the First Men Like Ourselves," section 1, p 70)

[17] Lemonick, Michael, "Odysseys of Early Man," *Time Magazine*, February 13, 1995, p. 40; "Stone-Age Bombshell," June 19, 1995, p. 57

[18] Hughes, Robert, "Behold the Stone Age," *Time Magazine*, February 13, 1995, p 38

[19] How conservative? To capture something of the flavor of this, consider that written history takes us back about five thousand years. Christianity is only two thousand years old. Yet in this area of western Europe a culture apparently endured relatively unchanged for some thirteen thousand years.

[20] Coon, *The Origin of Races*, Chapter 1 "The Problem of Racial Origins," Section "The Species Concept," p. 13; Chapter 11, Section "Continuity and Change in the Caucasoid Quadrant," p. 488; Section "The Meaning of the Mount Carmel Skeletons," pp. 573 - 575 (Here Coon points out that all the excitement was occasioned by the discovery of one skull, Skhul 5. Skhul 5 is described on pages 570 - 571); Dobzhansky, Theodosius, *Mankind Evolving* (Yale University Press, 1962), Chapter 7 "The Emergence of Man," Section "Monophyletic or Polyphyletic Origins," p. 191

[21] This thesis received further support from an attempt on the part of Matthias Krings, Anne Stone, Ralf W. Sctmitz, Heike Krainitzki, Mark Stoneking, and Svante Paabo to extract and analyze the DNA of a Neanderthal specimen found in western Germany in 1856 and believed to be between 30,000 and 100,000 years old. Their conclusions published in *Cell* (Vol. 90, July 11, 1997, pp. 19 - 30) suggest that the age of the common ancestor of Neanderthals and modern humans is four times greater than the age of the common ancestor of modern humans, that Neanderthals were a separate species, and that as a separate species they died out without contributing to the modern gene pool. This research was further substantiated when in March, 2000, an analysis was published in *Nature* of the DNA taken from the rib of a 29,000 year old skeleton of a two month old baby that had been buried in a cave in the Caucasus in Russia. Though there was a 3.5% difference between this sample and the older sample from Germany, both samples were approximately 7% different from the DNA of modern humans. This result has been confirmed in subsequent analyses.

[22] As reported on MSNBC April 1999.

[23] Zoeller-Greer, Peter, "Genesis, Quantum Physics and Reality. How the Bible agrees with Quantum Physics – an Anthropic Principle of Another Kind: the Divine Anthropic Principle," *Perspectives on Science and Christian Faith* (Vol 52, No. 1, March 2000), pp. 8 - 17

[24] Darwin, *The Origin of Species*, Chapter 4 "Natural Selection," pp. 70, 86,107, Chapter 6, pp. 152, 167 - 168, 171; Chapter 10 "On the Geological Succession of Organic Beings," p. 275; Chapter 11 Geographical Distribution," 291

[25] Ibid., Chapter 6, pp. 95, 108, 109

[26] Thus Darwin asserts the natural selection cannot produce absolute perfection (Chapter 6, pp 168, 171).   We should note that improvement must be understood contingently. By Darwin's standard the dinosaurs were far better adapted to their world than were the mammals since the dinosaurs proliferated far beyond the mammals, dominating them throughout the Mesozoic era. Indeed, had things remained as they were, the dinosaurs might dominate today. Mammals became an improvement only when conditions changed.

[27] Darwin used domesticated species as analogues for what he believed occurred in nature, a move which I think led to a fundamental conceptual mistake. His appeal to variation among domesticated   species   was   primarily   intended   to illustrate   the plasticity of species (Chapter 1, pp. 12, 27; Chapter 4, p. 68), but from that appeal Darwin extrapolated a move toward perfection which he based on breeders' efforts to derive "the best" from existing stock (Chapter 4, p. 86). Of course the question becomes, "The best for what?", and the answer is, "The best for the breeder's purposes." But nature, as understood by Darwin, is informed by principles not purposes, and therefore cannot strive toward a quality of perfection since such a quality implies something outside the contingent realm of material and secondary cause. It is this dimension of Darwin which, as we pointed out in the second chapter, Gleick, with some justification, sees as teleological However science qua science cannot test for teleology. Therefore, evolution theory to secure its status as science had to abjure the thesis that evolution is teleological and strives toward perfection.

[28] Ibid , Chapter 6, p 158

[29] The ability to interpret the meaning of symbols is not the same as intuition since no necessary meaning attaches to symbols while intuition is generally understood to refer to the ability to abstract necessary conclusions from apparently disparate data without benefit of formal logic.

[30] Darwin observed that "judgment or reason, often comes into play, even in animals very low in the scale of nature." (Chapter 7 "Instinct," p. 173). Of course Darwin's followers have long since abandoned the idea that animals can exercise any such qualities in favor of the idea that they act as robots, this despite that fact that to design robots that can mimic the simplest judgments made by these creatures is no easy task and has generally been unsuccessful.

[31] I distinguish here between location and mass. I can imagine that a soul, though it lacks mass, might be located in space in a way analogous to the way an idea, though located in language, is distinct from language.